Probate Made Simple

The essential guide to saving money and
getting the most out of your solicitor

by Andrew Komarnyckyj

HARRIMAN HOUSE LTD

3A Penns Road
Petersfield
Hampshire
GU32 2EW
GREAT BRITAIN

Tel: +44 (0)1730 233870
Fax: +44 (0)1730 233880
Email: enquiries@harriman-house.com
Website: www.harriman-house.com

First published in Great Britain in 2010
Reprinted with minor revisions

Copyright © Harriman House Ltd

The right of Andrew Komarnyckyj to be identified as author has been asserted
in accordance with the Copyright, Design and Patents Acts 1988.

ISBN: 978-1-9066-59554

Printed and bound in Great Britain by CPI Antony Rowe

Disclaimer

Please note that this book does not replace the need to take professional legal advice. It recommends that readers take professional legal advice whenever they undertake any probate work. It recommends that professional legal advice is taken by any reader thinking about acting on any of the issues mentioned, and that they take shelter under the expertise and indemnity cover of the solicitor they instruct to assist them.

The author does not accept responsibility for loss occasioned to any person acting, or failing to act, as a result of the content of this book.

Contents

Introduction

The purpose of this book is to provide legal clients with a practical guide to saving money on probate. It is brief and to the point in order to make it as user-friendly and as practical as possible.

The book makes the following assumptions about you and your aims:

- you need probate

- you are not a tax expert and have no desire to become one

- you are not a probate legal expert and have no desire to become one

- you want to avoid having to get to grips with technical legal jargon

- you want practical, risk-free advice

- you want to be shown how to save substantial amounts of money in the fewest possible words

- you are dealing with a probate in the legal jurisdiction of England and Wales (the advice given may not apply elsewhere).

As this is a book about saving money on probate fees, ancillary issues such as inheritance tax (IHT) are touched on where necessary but not explained in depth.

You will not need to be an expert to save money – you will simply need to know how to approach and make use of experts to help you where necessary.

Technical language has been avoided for the most part. However, if any words are used which you do not understand, please download the free publication 'Legal Jargon Buster' from www.willsprobateandmore.co.uk – which should provide you with the definitions that you require.

If you read this book and apply the principles it contains you are practically guaranteed to save substantial amounts of money in probate legal fees.

1. Understanding Probate – What Probate Means

If you want to save money on probate you will need to begin by understanding what probate is.

The word 'probate' is often used rather loosely to refer to the process of dealing with the financial affairs of someone who has died. Strictly speaking, probate is a document which you will need to access the money, property, bank accounts and other assets held in the name of a deceased person who has left a will.

The full name for this document is a Grant of Probate.

If the deceased person did not make a will, the document that you will need is called a Grant of Letters of Administration.

There are many different types of grant, but the Grant of Probate and Grant of Letters of Administration are the most commonly used types, and the only types that most people require. In the interests of simplicity, this book will use the word 'probate' for both types of grant, and for the process of dealing with the financial affairs of someone who has died.

You will find that once banks and other institutions are notified of the death of an account holder, they will freeze his accounts. The accounts will remain frozen until probate has been issued and has been sent to the banks. This often means that no money will be available until after probate has been obtained.

2. Probate in a Nutshell

The following steps are required for probate:

- register the death

- arrange the funeral

- pay the funeral bill

- value the money, property, assets and debts of the deceased

- prepare papers to apply for probate

- pay inheritance tax if applicable

- apply for probate

- get probate and cash the assets/obtain the money (i.e. send withdrawal forms to the banks, sell or transfer the house, etc)

- pay the debts of the deceased – e.g. credit card bills, outstanding income tax, etc

- pay any administration expenses (i.e. fees of professionals who have provided their services)

- prepare estate accounts

- distribute what is left to the person or persons entitled under the will (or under the rules of intestacy if there is no will).

This is not an exhaustive list, but serves to indicate the broad sweep of what is required.

3. Work That Does Not Require the Input of a Solicitor

Some probate work often does not require the input of a solicitor. Some of it does, depending on the circumstances. The work which often does not require input from a solicitor is:

- registering the death

- arranging the funeral

- paying the funeral bill

- valuing the money, property, assets and debts of the estate

- cashing the assets (i.e. sending withdrawal forms to the banks, arranging the sale of the house, etc)

- paying the debts of the deceased – e.g. credit card bills, outstanding income taxes, etc

- paying any administration expenses (i.e. fees of professionals who have provided their services)

- preparing estate accounts (if accounts are needed an accountant might be preferable to a solicitor)

- distributing what is left to the person or person entitled under the will (or under the rules of intestacy if there is no will).

All the above work is usually administrative in nature and can be done by anybody reasonably literate and numerate who is prepared to put in the time and effort.

You will note that this is the bulk of the work involved in probate. Much of it is what solicitors actually charge as much as £325 per hour to do.

4. Work That May Require the Input of a Solicitor

The work that it may be advisable to give to solicitors is:

- preparing the papers to apply for probate
- calculating the inheritance tax payable on an estate (if the estate is taxable)
- arranging payment of inheritance tax
- obtaining probate
- doing the conveyancing for the sale or transfer of the house (though you could equally consider a licensed conveyancer from whom you might get a better deal)
- advice on any trust issue that arises in your probate matter
- advice on any probate issue that you fail to understand
- any task you do not feel fully competent to deal with yourself.

5. Summary of Your Options

This section sets out the different options available to you. The remainder of the book explains the options in greater depth to enable you to carry them out and save money on legal fees.

If you have a probate matter, there are three options that you can follow to deal with it:

1. You can give it to a solicitor and ask him to do everything.

2. You can do some of the work yourself and employ a solicitor to help out with the legally-challenging aspects of the matter.

3. You can do it all yourself.

6. Pros and Cons of the Three Options

In order to choose the option that is right for you, you will need to have a clear idea of what you stand to gain and what the risks might be.

The following table provides this information.

Option 1: Giving the probate to a solicitor and asking him to do everything.

Pros	Cons
Minimal risk.	Potentially very high fees.
Minimal effort required on your part.	mPaying for non-legal work that you could do yourself.
Nothing should go wrong.	Potential difficulty in knowing what progress is being made.
If something does go wrong you may be able to recover compensation for losses.	Lack of control.

Possible deciding factors

• If you are named as executor but you do not receive any benefit from the estate, you might just as well give it to a solicitor to deal with as you will have nothing to lose (but it would probably still be a good idea to use the money-saving information contained in the next section if you do this)

- the estate may be large and/or complex and you may feel out of your depth taking on even part of the work yourself
- you may have an aversion to paperwork
- you may not want to do any of the work yourself
- you may be totally risk averse
- the estate may be insolvent, in which case you will not have a financial interest in it and may as well give it to a solicitor.

Option 2: Doing some of the work yourself and employing a solicitor to help out with the legally-challenging aspects of the matter.

Pros	Cons
Minimal risk.	Requires effort.
Save money on fees.	Risk of loss if you take on work that is beyond you (this book recommends that anything complex is given to your solicitor).
You will have control.	No compensation for your own mistakes (this book alerts you to many mistakes that might be made to enable you to check for them).
You will know what progress is being made without having to call your solicitor all the time.	
Risk of loss should be minimised if you delegate all work which requires legal expertise.	

Possible deciding factors

- You have a financial interest in the matter, i.e. you will receive money from the residue of the estate

- you are not averse to paperwork

- you have the time available to post letters, etc.

Option 3: Doing it yourself.

Pros	Cons
Save maximum money on fees.	Risk – possibly massive risks if you underestimate the complexity of the matter or overestimate your abilities.
You will have control.	Requires effort.
You will know what progress is being made without having to call a solicitor all the time.	Risk of loss if you take on work that is beyond you or make a mistake.
Many people successfully do probate on a DIY basis every year.	No compensation for your own mistakes.

Possible deciding factors

- You have a financial interest in the matter, i.e. you will receive money from the residue of the estate

- there is a will which is clear and easy to understand, or there is no will but it is clear who should inherit the estate

- the estate is a low-value estate and there is no possibility that inheritance tax will be charged

- everyone who will receive something from the estate is an adult and mentally capable.

7. Recommendation on Which Option to Choose

In some cases Option 1 is to be preferred. If the estate is insolvent (i.e. the debts exceed the money, property and assets) you could easily come unstuck if you tried to administer it yourself. Moreover, you would have nothing to gain financially. So if the estate is insolvent, Option 1 is recommended.

Similarly, if you are not a beneficiary and have no personal financial interest in the estate, you may feel it is reasonable to limit your involvement and give everything to a solicitor. Or if you are a beneficiary but only receive a fixed sum from the estate, or a percentage share of the estate, you may feel that a saving in legal fees, even if considerable, would not benefit you greatly.

If you choose Option 1 for these or almost any other reasons (except possibly that the estate is insolvent) you are still strongly recommended to follow the advice given in Section 8 to minimise the legal fees. Huge savings are possible if this advice is followed. And the beneficiaries of the estate will thank you for it.

The advice given in Section 8, really, is how to save money on probate the very easy way. It is (I believe) the preferred route for at least two-thirds of personal representatives.

If you have the time available to do some work yourself, and you are not averse to paperwork, then the recommendation of this book is that Option 2 would be the best option to take if you want to maximise your savings in probate legal fees. It will save you substantial amounts of money and provide a way forward that is as near risk-free as you are likely to get. It is not the easiest way to save money in probate, but the advice given together with the correspondence pack in Appendix 2 makes it about as easy as it could be.

Section 9 gives you a step-by step procedure to enable you to implement Option 2 successfully, and hence make massive savings.

Option 3 is clearly the way to make the biggest savings but is not recommended. If the estate is small, the issues are clear, and you have the time and inclination to get to grips with the official forms, it may be appropriate. However, if you choose Option 3 you are entirely on your own. You will have to be your own tax expert and your own legal expert.

Note that whatever savings you might make using Option 2 or Option 3, it is always worth considering Option 1. If you get a keen quote from a reputable solicitor, the effort and risks involved in making further savings may not seem worthwhile.

If you do wish to proceed with Option 2 and Option 3, there are free resources available at www.willsprobateandmore.co.uk which should be of assistance.

8. Saving Money if You Choose Option 1

Giving Everything to a Solicitor

8.1 Outline of Procedure

If you choose Option 1 and give the entire probate to a solicitor, there are ways of saving money on legal fees.

Purchasing legal expertise is similar to buying almost any other service. If you are after a keen price, you will not normally approach just one supplier of a service – you will approach a number of suppliers and ask them for a price quote.

Many people think that they are tied into using the solicitor who holds the will. This is not true. If you are named as the executor and the solicitor is not named as executor, you are free to choose whichever solicitor you like to deal with the probate.

So you should approach a number of solicitors with the details of the probate and ask them to give you a quote.

8.2 Choosing Which Solicitors to Approach

If your probate matter is straightforward and the estate is not a high-value estate, you are probably safe to approach any solicitors with demonstrable experience in probate work.

If the estate is complicated and/or high value, you are probably advised to approach only those solicitors with STEP members (the Society of Trust and Estate Practitioners).

If there is a dispute of some kind, you should approach firms of solicitors with ACTAPS members (the Association of Contentious Trust and Probate Specialists).

8.3 Trade Secrets – Forewarned is Forearmed

It will help you to know what solicitors may try to do, so that you know what to expect and what to ask for.

8.3.1 Estimated fees and percentage charging

The traditional way that solicitors inform you about their fees for probate is by means of an estimate. They will give you an hourly rate and an estimate of how many hours the job will take. If more hours are taken than were estimated, you will generally pay more than the original estimate.

The hours that solicitors estimate are not the hours to which you are accustomed. Solicitors work in units of six minutes. Every task is measured in six-minute periods, and any task that does not fit neatly into six-minute periods is rounded up to the nearest six minutes. So a one-minute task will cost you six minutes of your solicitor's time; a seven-minute task will cost you 12 minutes of his time. If a solicitor writes ten letters and takes one minute over each letter, he will charge you for an hour, not for ten minutes.

It is perfectly feasible for probate lawyers to write letters at the rate of one or more per minute, as many of their letters are pre-written standard letters which only require the insertion of a name and an address by a secretary.

In addition they will usually ask for a percentage of the value of the estate. The Law Society guidelines suggest percentage fees may be charged of 0.5% of the value of the dwelling house (home) of the deceased, and 1% of the value of all other assets. (However, if a solicitor is named as executor in a will, the guideline percentage fees are increased to 0.75% of the value of the dwelling house (home) of the deceased, and 1.5% of the value of all other assets.)

The Law Society guidelines are no more than guidelines and it is not unknown for solicitors to exceed them.

So the total charge you could pay for a probate matter could be an hourly rate probably ranging from £120 per hour plus VAT at the bottom end, to over £300 per hour plus VAT at the top end – *plus* a percentage fee of 0.5% (or more) of the dwelling house and 1% (or more) of all other assets.

If you are not careful, you will approach a number of solicitors and come away with estimates and agree to pay a percentage fee as well as an hourly rate. Those hours will not represent true hours worked; they will represent rounded-up hours.

What you must do is tell the solicitors you approach for quotes that you want a firm, fixed quote – not an estimate.

You must bear in mind that because probate solicitors are accustomed to charging a percentage of the value of the estate, many of them will take the view that they should charge far more for a high-value estate than for a low-value estate, even if little or no extra work is involved in the high-value estate. If you have a high-value estate, this may be reflected in the quotes that they give you, which may include a disproportionate premium just because high values are involved.

In order to reduce the possibility of percentage charges being secretly factored into the quotes that you are given, you should make it clear that you are obtaining a number of quotes. This will tend to focus the mind of the solicitor on giving a competitive quote. You could also ask the solicitor what his usual hourly rate is, and how many hours he thinks your matter will take. This should expose any quotes that are unreasonably inflated by percentage charging.

You should approach a number of solicitors on this basis – certainly at least three, possibly as many as five or more. Then you will be able to make an informed decision about who to give the probate to.

It is difficult to indicate to you what constitutes a reasonable quote for probate and what does not, as all probate matters are different. However, this book provides some information to help you.

If you refer to Table 1 and Table 2 in Appendix 1, you will find an illustration of the time it might normally take a solicitor to deal with a simple, straightforward probate matter where you have instructed him on the basis of Option 1. Table 1 illustrates solicitor's time (every task is measured in units of 6 minutes) and Table 2 illustrates real time (the time it actually takes to perform each task).

The extent to which solicitors need to charge six minutes when only one minute of time is used is debatable. Some firms of solicitors might be capable of making a profit when charging one minute for one minute of time used. Other less efficient firms may need to charge six minutes even when only one minute is used.

You might find that some solicitors will give you quotes on the basis indicated in Table 1, while others who are efficient, super competitive and really want the job will quote on the basis indicated in Table 2.

Remember that Tables 1 and 2 are given for illustrative purposes only, and are not intended as a general guide to the cost of probate.

Section 8.4.3 provides guidelines which should assist with determining whether the quotes you are given are competitive.

8.3.2 Transferable nil-rate band/Deeds of variation/Nil-rate band deeds

You may find that saving tax via something called the transferable nil-rate band is used to justify high quotes, and, on the face of it, this is very convincing.

Your solicitor, when he has looked through your papers, may tell you that he can make use of the transferable nil-rate band and thereby save you (say) £80,000 in inheritance tax. But due to the technicalities involved, this will add £X to your quote. As you are not a tax expert, you may be very impressed by this information and agree to the fee. After all, a saving of £80,000 may appear to be worth an additional fee of £X.

However, if you look on the HMRC website, you should be able to download a copy of the form used for the transferable nil-rate band. Without knowing anything about what it is or how it works, you should be able to satisfy yourself that if you supplied your solicitor with the information needed to complete the form, it would not take him very long to fill it in and send it to Her Majesty's Revenue & Customs (HMRC). Possibly less than an hour in many cases.

Some firms of solicitors have standard charges for certain products – e.g. they might have a standard charge of £1000 for all 'deeds of variation' or nil-rate band trust deeds. Straightforward deeds of variation should not generally cost this much as they do not take that much time to consider and produce – however impressive they may sound. (See Appendix 1, Table 5.)

Even a nil-rate band trust deed can also be produced fairly quickly if the solicitor is familiar with the task.

8.4 Detailed Advice on Obtaining Quotes

8.4.1 Ask the right questions and provide the right information

You should begin by obtaining a list of the solicitors in your area who do probate work. You could do this by looking on the internet or by contacting the Law Society.

You should telephone a number of them and ask to speak to a solicitor who works in the probate department.

Let the solicitor know that you have a probate matter and that you want to know how they charge for probate. In many cases you will be told that they charge on the basis of an hourly rate plus a percentage of the value of the estate. If this is the response that you receive, advise them that you are not prepared to pay a percentage fee and ask whether they would charge on the basis of an hourly rate alone. If the answer is that they would, you can ask whether they would be prepared to give you a definite fixed fee based on their hourly rate and an estimate of how many hours the matter will take. If the answer to this question is also positive, you could ask about the experience of the people who manage the department and/or whether they are STEP members. You could then arrange an appointment to visit them and obtain a quote.

You will need to give your solicitor adequate information to enable him to give you a meaningful quote. You should therefore obtain all the financial papers of the deceased, and separate them into different categories – bank accounts, shares, insurance policies, bills and so on.

When you have done this, you should compile a list of assets and a list of debts which you can give to your solicitor. You should provide approximate values if possible, as the value of the estate could make a difference to the quote.

If the estate is taxable, your solicitor will probably be involved in more complicated form filling than if it is not. He will probably also have to make more extensive enquiries. This will mean higher legal fees.

The documents that you obtain may not disclose the values of the money, property and assets. In such a case you could ask your solicitor to provide two quotes, one for if the estate is taxable, and one for if it is not. Alternatively, you could bite the bullet and obtain accurate values using the procedures outlined in Section 9 (9.1.16).

In addition to the list of assets and debts, you will need to give your solicitor the following information to enable him to quote:

• details of whether there is a will

- a copy of the will if there is one, or details of who is entitled to the estate if there is no will

- a copy of the death certificate

- details of whether the deceased made any gifts and if so a list of gifts as per Section 9.1.16

- details of the personal information as per Section 9.2.1

- when you give this information to the solicitors, you should ask whether there is anything else that they require in order to quote.

In most cases you should be able to give your solicitor the papers and copies of the lists that you have made. It should then be possible for him to prepare a quote, having perused the papers of the deceased during your meeting. On rare occasions it may be necessary to leave the papers with him. If this is the case, you should set a definite and short time limit – e.g. say you need to pick up the papers later the same day.

Remember that you will have to work with your solicitor and possibly be in contact with him over a long period, so the exercise is not just about obtaining a fair and reasonable quote for the work – it is also about determining whether you would feel comfortable working with the solicitor that you instruct. So you should be conscious of the impression that your solicitor makes on you during your initial meeting. This might influence whether you instruct him, irrespective of the quote that you are given.

If you have a large and complicated probate to deal with, it might be worth your while asking a probate broker to get you a quote. There is only one in the country at present: Adam Walker, of Final Duties. His website can be found at www.finalduties.co.uk. It is probably worth your while to look at his website, whether or not you plan on using his services, as it should reassure you that it is possible to tie solicitors down to reasonable fixed quotes (however much they might appear sometimes to resist this concept).

Please note that this does not represent an endorsement of Final Duties and that it is up to you to make your own enquiries to satisfy yourself that their service is good and worth paying for if you go down that route.

8.4.2 Understand what is involved

Even if you are planning on giving everything to a solicitor, there are some things that you will probably have to do yourself and cannot delegate – e.g. registering the death. You should therefore read the first few steps given in Section 9, as some of the advice may apply to you.

Moreover, in order to make sense of the quotes that you are given, it would help you to read the next section in its entirety, as it will inform you what your solicitor will actually be doing for his money. This is not essential, but it is desirable.

8.4.3 Good quote, bad quote

Andrew East, the chairman of the STEP probate committee, has stated that "solicitors' fees typically work out at around 3% of the value of an estate but fall to 1% to 2% in simple cases. Much of the cost will depend on the number of beneficiaries." (*The Guardian*, 9 September 2006.)

It can be stated with some certainty that if your quotes exceed the 'typical' figures suggested by Andrew East, they are on the high side and bad quotes.

In all probability you should be able to do better than the 'typical' figures. As an example chosen at random, there is a firm of solicitors advertising on the internet called Cooks Solicitors (www.cooks-solicitors.co.uk), which charges 1% of the value of the estate + VAT + out of pocket expenses (known as disbursements). Conveyancing fees incur an additional charge at the firm's usual conveyancing rates. Note that this is not an endorsement for Cooks Solicitors! This information is given merely to indicate that you can probably do better than Andrew East's quote suggests.

Another website worth looking at in your quest to obtain a competitive quote is Winston Solicitors (www.probate-law.co.uk/prices). Their fixed fee of £1,495 + VAT + disbursements + conveyancing on any estate within the nil-rate band, or any estate below £624,000 where it is possible to make use of a deceased spouse's nil-rate band, represents very good value where an estate has significant assets. Again, this is not an endorsement! It is merely cited as another indicator of what is possible within the probate legal marketplace.

You will need to be aware that 1% + VAT can be a very good, very competitive quote in some cases, but not in others. If the estate has a total value of £20,000 and consists of a dozen bank accounts and a hundred or so shares then a quote of 1% + VAT + disbursements is very competitive indeed. I would personally probably accept it rather than do the work myself. If the estate has a total value of £200,000 and consists of just one bank account, then a quote of 1% + VAT is not remotely competitive. Table 2 in Appendix 1 will indicate to you how much work the lawyer would be doing to earn his or her money in that scenario. Not much!

In order to evaluate your quotes you will certainly need to compare them. In addition it would help you to familiarise yourself with the probate process as set out in Section 9, and Tables 1 and 2 in Appendix 1. These should help you to get a feel for the amount of work involved in your matter.

A good quote in many cases will not exceed 1% + VAT of the value of the estate + conveyancing + disbursements. And in some cases it may be considerably less.

However, if the estate is of modest value but includes a large number of assets then 1% + VAT may represent an unrealistically low figure for legal fees.

Table 5 in Appendix 2 may help you to make sense of the quotes that you receive – but the information it contains should not be used in isolation; it should be considered in conjunction with the other information given in this book. And it should be considered as no more than a very rough guide.

If the quotes you receive all appear to be high, this could indicate that your matter is more complex than you appreciate; or it could indicate that in your area solicitors are unaccustomed to being competitive. You should therefore ask for justification before proceeding – ask how many hours the solicitors think your matter will require; and ask why it will take so long if their estimate of this is considerably different to yours. (There could be a valid reason – your estate might include something potentially very time-consuming of which you are unaware.)

If you take these steps, you should be in a position to instruct a solicitor on the basis of Option 1 knowing that you have done everything possible to ensure that the charges are fair and reasonable and known in advance.

8.5 Saving Money by Using Option 2

Section 9 consists of a step-by-step guide to saving money by using Option 2. It is a general guide for all probate matters. It may well include steps which are not relevant to your particular probate matter. You should simply ignore the irrelevant steps when you encounter them and move on to the next one.

Before you begin work, you should read through all the steps to make sure that you have in mind a complete picture of what is required.

8.5.1 General approach

You need to be aware of the general approach advocated by this book. You are not encouraged to take on any probate work unless you want to – two-thirds of all individuals apparently do not want to do probate work themselves, and would rather give the work to a professional. If you fall into this group, then use Option 1 and refer to the remainder of this book purely to help you to assess the quotes that you receive from solicitors.

If you belong in the minority of approximately one-third who want to self-administer estates, then the remainder of this book should prove invaluable to you.

The approach you are encouraged to take is a safety-first approach – you should do only those tasks which require common sense rather than in-depth legal knowledge, and only do them provided that you understand what you are doing and the risk is therefore minimal.

Anything that you do not understand or which requires any kind of expertise should be given to your solicitor so that he can apply his expertise to the problem. You can then take advantage of the protection of the indemnity insurance cover your solicitor will have.

This book will point out the risks to help you to avoid them – if you take legal advice! As you are being called on to do administrative work rather than legal work, risks should only arise from simple mistakes which you should be able to watch out for and eliminate, provided you take care and check your own work. If you have a co-executor who is helping, you should both be able to work together and check for errors.

8.5.2 Deciding how much to do yourself – guidelines

Please refer to the following table for guidelines you should consider, and ensure that you read and understand all the steps in Section 9 before you decide what work you should delegate to your solicitor and what work you should do yourself.

Your Knowledge/Situation	What You Should Consider
You understand the will, or there is no will but you understand who will benefit from the estate. You have seen the financial documents and they are all straightforward and you understand them. Everyone who will benefit is an adult who is mentally capable. There are no trusts in the will.	You should be able to do everything in this section from stage 1 through to the final stage.
You do not understand the will or do not understand who will benefit from the estate. You have seen the financial documents and they are all straightforward and you understand them.	You should be able to carry out stages 1, 2 and 3 successfully. You would be advised to delegate the other stages to your solicitor.
You understand the will or there is no will but you understand who will benefit from the estate. You have seen the financial documents and some of them are beyond you. Everyone who will benefit is an adult who is mentally capable. There are no trusts in the will.	You should be able to do everything in this section from stage 1 through to the final stage. However, you would be well-advised to delegate to your solicitor the stage 3 work relating to all the financial products that you do not understand, or at the very least to discuss them with him.
You do not understand the will or do not understand who will benefit from the estate. You have seen the financial documents and they are all straightforward and you understand them. / You have seen the financial documents and some of them are beyond you.	You should be able to carry out stages 1 and 2 successfully. You would be advised to delegate the other stages to your solicitor.
There is a dispute over the estate.	Discuss the matter with your solicitor. You should be able to carry out stages 1 to 3. Depending on whether and how the dispute is resolved, and whether you understand the will etc, you may be able to carry out the other stages including the final stage.

9. Saving Money if You Choose Option 2

Doing Some of the Work Yourself and Giving the Legally-Challenging Work to a Solicitor: a Step-by-Step Guide

---

9.1 First Stage: Work up to Probate

9.1.1 Make sure that you are the person or one of the persons with the right to administer the estate

Before you do anything, make sure that you are entitled to do it! This means that you must be either the executor named in a will, or, if there is no will, one of the persons entitled under the rules of intestacy. If in doubt, consult with a solicitor to find out what your rights are.

Provided that you are satisfied that you are an executor or administrator, you can proceed.

9.1.2 If there is no will – a warning!

If you knew the deceased well, you may be able to say with certainty that no will was ever made. However, you need to be aware of the dangers of getting it wrong, and what you can do to protect yourself. The dangers are that if you incur any expenses – e.g. on solicitor's fees – you will not have a right to be reimbursed from the estate. You will be personally liable to pay the solicitor's fees.

Worse still, if you go so far as to distribute an estate on the basis that there is no will, and a will subsequently turns up, this could lead to losses and a claim against you for a substantial sum of money. Similar dangers exist even where there is a will, if a later will was also made.

Rather than take this risk, if you have any doubts at all about the true position, you are advised to make a thorough search for a will.

Obvious steps to take include making a thorough search of the papers of the deceased, speaking to people who knew the deceased, contacting all the solicitors/will-writers in the areas where the deceased may have lived, and checking whether the bank of the deceased has anything in safe custody. You could also try the Probate Service and some of the professional will storage companies.

If you want to give yourself real protection against the possibility of financial loss, you are probably advised to organise a professional search for a will by a specialist company such as Title Research (www.titleresearch.com). It may cost you money in order to do so.

The advantage of using Title Research is that they will produce a report which you can use to obtain insurance cover to protect yourself against the risk that a will might be found.

You may be able to persuade Title Research to make a search and prepare a report on the basis that you will pay them from the estate if the search confirms that you are the person authorised to deal with it – and they should look to the estate for payment if you are not the person authorised to deal with it. Title Research will not have a right to claim their fees from the estate and may not agree to such an arrangement, having had their fingers burnt by such arrangements in the past. You will just have to consult with them to find out what they are prepared to do and possibly take a view on whether you prefer to pay their fees or take a risk.

9.1.3 If there is a will – a warning!

If there is a will, you need to be sure that the will you are dealing with is the latest (i.e. most recent) will made by the deceased.

If you knew the deceased well, you may know for certain that you have the most recent will. If there is any doubt, you should carry out the same searches as those outlined in section 9.1.2 and give consideration to the use of Title Research (as suggested in 9.1.2).

9.1.4 Act within time limits, especially those of HMRC

Time limits to be aware of from the outset are:

A few weeks/months – property

If there is a property which was rented by the deceased, or anything else on which rent was being paid (e.g. berthing fees for a boat) any delay in resolving matters could lead to unnecessary charges being footed by the estate.

A few weeks/months – cars, shares, volatile investments

If there is a car in the estate, or other assets which appear to be depreciating (e.g. shares in a falling market), even a short delay could lead to a big depreciation in the value of the car or other assets.

Six months – tax implications

If there is inheritance tax to pay, interest will begin to accrue on unpaid inheritance tax as of six months from the date of death.

One year – tax implications

If there is inheritance tax to pay, details of the estate will need to be submitted to HMRC within 12 months of the date of death. If you fail to observe this time limit, without a reasonable excuse, HMRC can fine you up to £200.

One year – other implications

After one year, beneficiaries can call on personal representatives to distribute any part of the estate.

Two years – tax implications

If there is a further 12 months delay, HMRC can fine you up to a further £3000 and there may be other worse losses.

9.1.5 Secure the house/take meter readings

If the deceased owned a house or flat which is now empty, make sure that it is secure to prevent break-ins which could cause losses to the estate. Make sure that all doors and windows are shut and locked. It might even be necessary with some properties in some areas to have external steel shutters put over the windows to secure the house. You will have to be the judge of that.

It might also be a good idea to turn off the water, particularly in winter, to prevent damage in the event of a burst pipe.

Take readings from gas/water/electric meters as this information will be required later.

9.1.6 Make sure the house is insured to the full rebuilding value

If you fail to do this, the inheritance could literally go up in smoke.

You will need to look amongst the financial documents of the deceased and check whether there is an existing household buildings policy. If there is, you should telephone the insurance company, tell them about the changed circumstances, and ask if the cover can be maintained. Usually this will be possible; it may involve a number of conditions (such as visiting the property weekly and keeping a log of your visits).

If there is no existing policy, you will need to get one. You will find that cover for an unoccupied property is not easy to obtain. You could try insurance brokers and (surprisingly) solicitors for this type of insurance.

You should only insure the property if it was owned by the deceased. Moreover, you need to be aware that if the deceased owned a flat, and service charges were paid, it may not be necessary to pay for insurance cover; buildings insurance would probably be provided under the terms of the lease.

9.1.7 Remove all financial documents, cash, personal papers (such as birth and marriage certificates) and valuables to a place of safekeeping

These are all essential items which you will need to protect.

Make sure that the financial documents that you remove include all recent gas/electric/water/council tax/credit card bills and any other bills.

9.1.8 Rented houses/flats

If the deceased rented their home the estate will be responsible for paying the rent until the keys have been handed back to the landlord. There might be an additional requirement that the house should be cleared before the keys are handed back and the liability to pay rent ceases.

You should check with the landlord whether the house has to be cleared, then arrange clearance and hand in the keys as soon as possible.

If you fail to do this, significant amounts of money could be lost in the payment of rent unnecessarily.

You must make sure that you do not dispose of anything that is given away to a beneficiary of the will. You must also be sure that you are not disposing of anything of value which could be sold to raise money on behalf of the estate.

You must also make sure that you get a valuation of the contents before you clear the property. (Refer to the section on valuations.)

9.1.9 Arrange the funeral

That is, if you are a family member and/or it is expected of you or agreed that you should arrange it. You should be able to obtain expert guidance from a funeral director for this.

You should always check whether the estate has the funds to pay for the funeral before you arrange it. When you arrange the funeral, you are making a contract with the funeral director. Under that contract, you will be personally liable to pay for the funeral – if the estate is unable to do so.

If there are insufficient funds in the bank of the deceased (but funds elsewhere, e.g. tied up in a house) you will need to inform the funeral director that he may have a considerable wait before he can be paid – unless you elect to pay the bill from your own funds.

If you do arrange the funeral it is likely you will also have to register the death.

Arranging the funeral is not technically part of the duties of an executor, but he does have a duty to dispose of the body and a right to its custody and possession until disposal.

If the deceased left written directions that their body should be used for medical education or research (including written directions in their will) the person with lawful possession of the body may authorise the use of the body in accordance with that request, provided he has no reason to believe that the request was withdrawn.

This applies if the request was not written, but verbal, made during the deceased's last illness, and made in the presence of two witnesses.

9.1.10 Register the death

(a) Entitlement/time limits

Firstly, make sure that you are the person responsible for registering the death. There is a list of persons set out by law who have the responsibility for registering a death. The person with responsibility for registering the death (known as the 'informant') is usually a relative of the deceased. So if you are a close relative you will usually be able to register the death – but may wish to check with the Register Office first.

If no relative comes forward to register the death, the duty may be discharged by the occupier of the house in which the death occurred; or by anyone living in the house who knew about the death. If the death took place in an institution, the person on whom the duty falls is the senior resident officer.

Finally, the duty may fall on the person responsible for making the funeral arrangements.

So it is possible that if you are not a family member, the responsibility to register a death will fall on you if you are named as executor in a will, and as executor you are responsible for arranging the funeral.

If you ever find yourself in the position of having to register a death, you will need to read the documentation carefully prior to making an appointment with the Register Office. This is because you will need to make yourself aware of the information needed by the Register Office, as well as, if possible, obtaining the documents containing this information.

If you find that there is some information that is asked for that you simply cannot get hold of, the Register Office will usually accept that state of affairs and permit you to register the death without the information, provided you have made all reasonable enquiries (i.e. gone through the paperwork and contacted any friends or neighbours of the deceased for whom you have contact details, and who may be able to shed light on the matter).

Your funeral director and/or local registry office will advise on registering the death.

Bear in mind the time limits: the death should be registered within five days of its occurrence but an extension of a further nine days is permitted provided that the local Registrar of Births and Deaths has received written confirmation that a medical certificate giving the cause of death has been signed by a doctor.

The death must be registered in the sub-district in which the death occurred or the body was found. The address should be available from the telephone directory or internet.

(b) Number of death certificates needed

Your will need to obtain a sensible number of copies of the death certificate from the registrar. This usually means one for each financial institution, i.e. one for each bank, insurance company, investment company and so on used by the deceased.

(c) Notify the DWP of the death

One of the certificates that you receive from the registry office will be specifically for the purpose of informing the DWP of the death.

9.1.11 Pay the funeral bill

Many people pay the funeral bill themselves, then wait to be reimbursed from the estate. However, if there is sufficient money in a bank or building society account held by the deceased, this is not necessary. Simply send the funeral bill to the bank or building society with a covering letter, or hand the bill in over the counter, and the bank or building society will usually pay it.

Often the task of paying the funeral bill is undertaken by the solicitor, with a charge for his time. So this exercise is a procedure that will save you money.

(See precedent letter 1 in Appendix 2.)

9.1.12 Get hold of the original will

Make sure you have the original will. The chances are that you will need the death certificate in order to do this. You will need to send a copy of the death certificate to the solicitors (or other institution) holding the original will, together with a covering letter.

It is probably best to collect the will in person so as not to risk having it lost in the post. If circumstances oblige you to have it posted, make sure that it is sent by some secure method.

(See precedent letter 2 in Appendix 2.)

9.1.13 Read the original will and note the contents

Read the original will and make sure that you understand it. It may help you to keep the provisions in mind if you summarise it in your own words.

If there is anything that you do not understand, confer with a solicitor to ensure that you are not in danger of venturing out of your depth.

9.1.14 Redirect the post

Visit the post office and arrange to have all post redirected to your own address.

9.1.15 Open a probate bank account

Unless you are the only person entitled to the estate, it will be unwise to pay the money from the estate directly into your own bank account. Even if you are the only person entitled to the estate, it may still be unwise to pay the money from the estate directly into your own bank account if the estate is large and complicated. With a large and complicated estate you will need to keep track of everything for tax purposes and this will be easier if you have a separate account for the estate money.

You should visit the bank of your choice and open an executor's account in readiness for when you begin to receive the money from the estate.

9.1.16 Read through the financial documents and value the money, property and assets

In order to obtain probate, you will need to know the value of the estate. This involves getting hold of valuations of all the bank accounts, insurance policies, shares and all other assets.

There are some points you need to be aware of – these are generally addressed in the correspondence pack given in Appendix 2.

It is important to be aware that the values you require are the values of each asset on the date of death of the deceased. After the date of death those values could have changed – interest could have been added to bank accounts; shares could have risen or fallen in value. These changes do not have any bearing on the value for probate purposes, which is the value at the date of death.

Obtaining valuations is one of the areas in which you can make big savings in legal fees. Solicitors usually undertake this work, but they are no more qualified than you to do it and it requires no special expertise, (although you will have to call in the same experts that a solicitor would use). Obtaining valuations and being paid high hourly rates for the work really is money for old rope, especially when that rate is based on solicitors' time and not real time.

You should begin by putting the documents that you have into different categories – bank accounts, shares, insurance policies and so on. When you have done this, you should compile a list which you can use to keep track of your correspondence with the financial institutions. You should record on the list the name of each bank and insurance company etc, the date that you write to them, the date that you receive their reply, and the value given in their reply. You should also note whether each bank account (and every other asset) is the sole property of the deceased or jointly held with someone else.

You could consider getting some paper wallet files and opening a separate file for each asset, or each category of asset. Or you could use a lever arch file with card dividers and plastic wallets to retain the original documents.

Whatever system you adopt, it must be a system that enables you to keep track of everything and to see the results at a glance.

(a) Financial advisors/accountants

If the deceased was known to have consulted an independent financial advisor (IFA) and/or accountant, you should always contact the advisor for information about the finances of the deceased.

(*See precedent letter 3 in Appendix 2.*)

(b) Bank and building society accounts

To establish the value of the estate at the date of death for probate purposes you will need to write to all the banks and other financial institutions holding money and investments on behalf of the deceased. You should also consider checking whether any items are held in safe custody for the deceased.

(*See precedent letter 4 in Appendix 2.*)

(c) Insurance policies

You will need to value all insurance policies held in the name of the deceased.

Sometimes insurance policies are written in trust. You do not need to know what this means – you simply need to know that these should be referred to your solicitor for interpretation.

(See precedent letter 5 in Appendix 2.)

(d) Stocks and shares – plcs

If the estate includes shareholdings, your options are:

- value them yourself, or
- have them valued by a stockbroker.

It is probably essential to have them valued by a stockbroker if there is any possibility that inheritance tax will be at stake. If you value the shares yourself you should first register the death with the company registrars and ask them to confirm the number of shares held by the deceased. Failure to check on the number of shares held could result in an incorrect return being sent to HMRC; and, in the worst case scenario, a fine.

You will find the name and address details for the company registrars on the share certificates, but these cannot be relied upon, particularly with old share certificates. Before writing, you should therefore check the up-to-date details of the registrars. If you search the company name on the internet, you should be able to get these.

(See precedent letters 6 and 7 in Appendix 2; or if you are very uncertain about the information you have on the shareholdings, but the deceased was known to have used a stockbroker, you could resort to precedent letter 3.)

If there are many shareholdings and you despair of writing to all the registrars, you could instruct a stockbroker to confirm the number of shares, register the death with the registrars and provide a valuation.

You should discuss fees with the registrars before using their services.

(*See precedent letter 8 in Appendix 2.*)

If it emerges that the deceased held shares for which some share certificates are missing, and it is likely that these shares will need to be sold as soon as possible, you should obtain a document called a letter of indemnity from the registrars for completion so that the shares can be sold or transferred when the probate to the estate has issued. (It will not be possible to sell or transfer them without the probate.)

(e) Houses, flats and apartments

If there is a house, flat or land you will require a valuation or valuations. If inheritance tax is not an issue, an estimate based on similar properties for sale in the area may be adequate. If inheritance tax could be at stake, a professional valuation would be advisable.

The HMRC guidance includes the statement that "[y]ou do not have to get the property professionally valued, but you must take all reasonable steps to put a value on the property." (p.68 of the 'Guide to completing your Inheritance Tax account').

If the house is to be sold you will usually be instructing an estate agent and obtaining a professional valuation, so you might as well rely on this.

If you are the executor named in a will, you are entitled to instruct an estate agent to put the house up for sale at this stage – but you will not be able to exchange contracts until you have obtained probate.

If there is no will but you are one of the persons entitled to the estate, then strictly speaking you are not allowed to even put the house up for sale until probate has been obtained.

(f) Joint property

When bank accounts and shares are held jointly they usually become the property of the surviving joint owners. When you show a death certificate to the bank, or share registrar, this will usually be all that is required to transfer the account to the surviving joint holder.

You will still need to obtain valuations, as the value at the date of death of the deceased's half-share will have to be disclosed for probate purposes.

Similar rules apply to jointly owned houses or flats, except that you will find that it may be less likely that the surviving joint owner will inherit the half share of the deceased joint owner. The person who will inherit depends on whether the house or flat was held as joint tenants or tenants in common (if you wish to look this up, refer to the free legal jargon buster at www.willsprobateandmore.co.uk).

(g) Pension/salary etc

You will need to find out whether any pension (or salary) was owing to the deceased at the date of death, or whether there has been an overpayment which needs to be refunded by the estate.

If arrears of a pension or salary are owed to the estate, the arrears count as an asset which increases the value of the estate for probate purposes. If the deceased received an overpayment of salary or pension, this amounts to a debt which reduces the value of the estate for probate purposes.

(*See precedent letters 9-13 in Appendix 2.*)

(h) Unknown money, property and assets

It is possible that the person who died had money or assets for which there is no paperwork, as a result of which you may end up getting less than you should do from the estate. You can do a fairly extensive search to check for the existence of such assets using unclaimed assets facilities (www.uar.co.uk; www.unclaimedassets.co.uk).

(i) Complex financial instruments

A complex financial instrument for these purposes is any asset of any kind that you do not understand, and any trust. You may be able to make enquiries about the value of the financial instrument from the company that produced it, but in keeping with the philosophy of this book, if you do so, you should ensure that your solicitor has access to all the relevant papers at the appropriate time.

(j) House contents

The house contents and all other possessions of the deceased such as personal effects and jewellery are assets which contribute towards the value of the estate for probate purposes.

If there is anything of value, such as jewellery, antiques or paintings, these items will need valuing if only to ensure that when they are sold you get what they are worth. Even if there appears to be nothing of value in the property, a valuation by an auctioneer/valuer is advisable before you dispose of anything.

You need to be aware that if you are not the only beneficiary of the estate, one of the other beneficiaries could question the value of the house contents at a later stage and allege that you have disposed of them for less than their true value. You may wish to consider obtaining a written valuation, even if you think that one is not required, in order to pre-empt criticism of this kind.

(k) Cars

Antique cars should be valued by an appropriate expert, and the DVLA informed of the death. Insure cars if necessary.

(l) Business and agricultural interests, partnership interests and private limited company shares

The principles of valuing these assets are not dissimilar to the principles of valuing all the other assets in an estate. The assets are to be valued at the market value at the date of death. The only real difference is that the value for inheritance tax (IHT) purposes may be reduced by business property relief (BPR) or agricultural property relief (APR).

You will not need to become an expert on inheritance tax or on these varieties of relief. You need merely to know that they exist, and to ask the right person whether they apply to the assets in the estate.

If you are valuing a business or an interest in a business, a farm, or shares in a private limited company, then the best person to make the valuation is in many cases the accountant who prepared the accounts for the business, company or farm. He may also be the best person to ask on the issue of business and/or agricultural property relief – but I would suggest that this is probably only the case if he is a fully qualified accountant and carries indemnity insurance. You will have to check on these issues. If the person who does the accounts is not a fully qualified accountant, you would be advised to source a qualified, insured accountant capable of carrying out the valuations. It may be that an estate agent's input is required if the business includes land, and an estate agent will certainly be required if a farm is involved.

It would be wise to ask for the opinion of your solicitor on the issues of BPR and APR if they arise.

(*See precedent letter 3 in Appendix 2.*)

(m) Other money, property and assets not listed above

If there is any form of asset not listed above, this does not mean that you can ignore it; the asset must be valued as at the date of death in the same way as all other assets. If in doubt, raise the issue with your solicitor.

(n) Inheritance tax – gifts of property

If the deceased made gifts of money, property or other assets these could create a liability to inheritance tax (IHT). You will therefore need to obtain information about the gifts made by the deceased.

The rules relating to gifts are rather complicated. If you do not want to get to grips with tax law, then the only safe course of action is to list all gifts made by the deceased in the seven years prior to death totalling over £3000 in value in any one year, and to leave it to your solicitor to decide which gifts matter.

Note that for these purposes the word 'gifts' is very wide and includes:

- all direct gifts of money, property or other assets from one person to another

- all direct gifts of money, property or other assets from one person to a trust

- all sales of property for less than the market value if the property was not sold on the open market (e.g. if a parent sold a house to a child for less than the market value)

- granting a lease at less than the full market value

- re-arranging the shares in a private limited company

- agreeing to act as guarantor for someone else's debts

- paying premiums on a life assurance policy for someone else's benefit.

For each gift your list should include details of the date on which the gift was made, the nature of the gift (e.g. whether it was cash, shares, etc) the value of the gift, the name and address of the recipient, and their relationship to the deceased.

To obtain details of gifts you will need to check the papers of the deceased, make enquiries of their family and possibly friends, and his accountant and solicitors if applicable. Most estates will not have gift issues to deal with, certainly not complicated ones, and you will either be spared the task of compiling such a list, or the task will be straightforward.

If you do have to compile a list and it is obvious that it includes some difficult items (e.g. re-arrangement of shares) you will need to ensure that these are drawn to the attention of your solicitor and that either he or an accountant is responsible for providing a valuation.

(o) Income tax

You will need to find out whether the deceased owed any income tax at the date of death, or whether he had overpaid income tax at the date of death and was due a refund. If income tax is owed to the estate, the refund that is due counts as an asset which increases the value of the estate for probate purposes. If the deceased paid insufficient tax on his income and owed income tax at the date of death, this amounts to a debt which reduces the value of the estate for probate purposes.

All the precedent letters contain questions about the deceased's income where appropriate, to assist you to obtain the required information.

However, please note:

- you will find that some financial institutions are very efficient and will read your valuation letters carefully and provide all the information requested; others may initially supply only part of the information – usually a valuation at the date of death. You will then have to chase them up for the income information that is needed to deal with the income tax affairs of the deceased

- if the papers of the deceased do not indicate how much income has been received in the form of share dividends and you are not using a stockbroker, you will have to contact the share registrars directly for details of the share dividends received prior to the date of death. There is no precedent letter given for this, but it should be a simple matter for you to adapt one of them for this purpose.

(p) Capital gains tax (CGT)

In most estates, particularly small estates, CGT will not be an issue – but this does not mean that it can be entirely ignored.

You do not need to be a tax expert to find out what the CGT position is – you simply need to know what questions to ask, and then give the information that you obtain to your accountant. You should make enquiries to establish what the position is to ensure that you do not cost the estate (and yourself) money.

CGT is charged when an individual sells or gives away an asset. It is not charged on gifts of cash and some other assets.

It is charged on the gain in value (if any) between the date on which the asset was acquired and the date on which it was disposed of (i.e. sold or gifted). There is an annual exempt amount of gain on (in 2009-10) £10,100 for individuals. So it will only crop up if significant disposals of assets have been made. If they have, you could visit the HMRC website for further information.

If unpaid CGT could be an issue, you will need to make a list of disposals of assets made by the deceased, but this list need not go back further than three years (however, check this three-year limit with your advisor).

Your list should provide details of the asset/item of property sold (e.g. whether it was a house or shares, etc), the date of sale of each asset/item of property, the sale price, the date it was purchased by the deceased and the purchase price.

Your accountant will be able to go through the list and advise you of the CGT position and let you know whether more information is required.

9.1.17 Get on top of the income tax and CGT situation at an early stage

Inform HMRC of the death. When you have received your replies back from the banks etc, you will have details of the income of the deceased in the final year of his life. There may have been an overpayment of income tax to claim, or there may be a refund of income tax due to the estate.

You will also have made enquiries and (if applicable) compiled a list of gifts and sales made by the deceased, which may indicate a CGT liability.

The best person to deal with these issues is probably the accountant of the deceased if he had one. If he did not have an accountant, visit an accountant of your choice (or more than one) and ask for a quote on resolving the tax position up to the date of death. Or resolve it yourself if competent to do so.

An accountant should be able to work out fairly quickly whether the estate owes income tax or is due a refund of income tax, and provide you with a figure for this. This figure should be included on your list of assets (if a refund is due) or debts (if unpaid income tax is owed to HMRC).

Similarly, if your enquiries have revealed that the deceased made significant sales or gifts of anything on which there was unpaid CGT, this should be included on your list of debts.

9.1.18 Find out what is owed

You will need to know what debts were owed by the deceased. You should begin with the bills collected from the home of the deceased. You will need to make a list of the creditors, then write to them notifying them of the death, advising them to send future correspondence to you, and asking where appropriate for an up-to-date statement of the liability. You should inform them that payment will be made when funds become available.

(*See precedent letters 14-16 in Appendix 2.*)

9.1.19 List and contact the beneficiaries

Make a list of the beneficiaries who will inherit the estate and give details in your list of the item or share of the estate to which they are entitled. If the only beneficiaries are you and one or two other people who you know well, an informal telephone call or letter may be adequate to let them know that they are due to inherit something. If the beneficiaries are not known to you, it is advisable to put the matter on a formal footing by notifying them in a letter requesting evidence of their identity.

It is the usual practice that when a beneficiary is given a gift of property or a specific sum of money, he should be notified in a letter. If the beneficiary is given a share of the residue of the estate and there is a will, it is the usual practice to enclose a copy of the will with the letter.

It is not mandatory to inform beneficiaries in this way; it is optional. It will probably create better relationships with them than not contacting them until a later stage.

However, if you write to the beneficiaries at this stage, you must be sure that the information that you are giving them is correct. If you cannot be certain that you understand the contents of the will (or the distribution of the estate if there is no will), you should postpone writing to the beneficiaries until after you have met with a solicitor and received advice on the disposition of the estate.

(*See precedent letters 17-20 in Appendix 2.*)

9.1.20 Maintain records

By now you will have written to all the banks, building societies, etc, to all known creditors, and to the beneficiaries.

You will need to make sure that as you receive the replies you note the contents and file them in order.

9.2 Second Stage: Applying for Probate Via a Solicitor

9.2.1 Obtaining quotes

When you have received and noted the replies from the banks, insurance companies, creditors and so forth, you should have a file which will enable your solicitor to quote for the work that you want him to do.

You should refer again to the guidelines at the beginning of Section 9 and read through every step in Section 9, then take a view on what work you want to delegate to your solicitor, and what work you want to do yourself. You should also read through the advice given in Section 8, as much of this will be relevant.

When you visit your solicitor you should provide him with:

- the original papers belonging to the deceased (though you do not have to duplicate information)

- a copy of the will if there is one

- your list of the values of the money, property and assets

- your list of debts

- your list of beneficiaries giving details of what they are due to receive from the estate.

In addition, you should provide him with a separate list containing the following personal information relating to the deceased:

- the deceased's National Insurance number

- the deceased's tax reference

- the deceased's place of birth

- details as to whether the deceased's permanent home was located within England and Wales and how long it had been within England and Wales. If the deceased's permanent home was not obviously located within England and Wales, the matter will require discussion as there may be tax and other implications

- the deceased's marital status

- details of whether the deceased was survived by a spouse or civil partner, brothers or sisters, parents, children or grandchildren (and the number of children/grandchildren if applicable)

- the deceased's last known permanent address

- details of whether the deceased's last known permanent address was owned or part-owned by the deceased or whether the deceased had a right to live there

- details of whether anyone acted under a power of attorney granted by the deceased during his lifetime.

You should explain to your solicitor what work you have already done and explain what further work you propose doing. The very least that you will want your solicitor to quote for is the application for probate and the resolution of any inheritance tax issues.

If there is a house to sell or transfer, you will want him to quote separately for the conveyancing work. Likewise, if there is advice about tax planning to be given, you will want him to quote separately for that.

There are three objectives to this exercise:

1. To obtain a firm fixed quote.

2. To aim to use the solicitor's skills and indemnity insurance cover to protect you as far as possible from any risk.

3. To form an opinion on whether you would feel comfortable working with the solicitor, possibly over a long period.

Your solicitor's training has prepared him to advise and carry out complex legal tasks. This is what you are expecting of him – not administrative work and routine correspondence that you can do for yourself.

If you are very confident and well informed, and the estate is straightforward, you may want your solicitor to restrict his work to obtaining a grant of probate for you, and you may wish to do everything else without any guidance or help. Alternatively, you may take a safety-first approach (recommended in most cases) and tell your solicitor that the work for which he is quoting will include any or all of the following:

- looking through the papers of the deceased and checking them against your lists of assets and liabilities to make sure that you have not overlooked anything

- confirming that your list of assets correctly states whether the assets are the sole property of the deceased or jointly owned as far as can be disclosed from the paperwork

- confirming that your list of beneficiaries is correct and that you have correctly stated what they should receive from the estate

- providing written advice on whether a deed of variation or tax planning arrangement should be considered; and if so providing a quote for carrying out the deed of variation/tax planning

- providing written advice as to whether there are any issues not referred to above which could complicate administering the estate

- providing written advice on any issues that you do not understand (explain what, if any, these issues are)

- advising you in writing of any enquiries you should make that you have not made, e.g. bankruptcy searches.

And, if you are planning on carrying out the third stage yourself,

- providing written advice on whether any adverse consequences could arise from cashing in and transferring the assets and whether any action should be considered to mitigate capital gains tax before you proceed

- providing written advice on whether you can safely pay all the debts from the money that you obtain from the banks, etc.

You should put this in writing to your solicitor to formalise the arrangement, and to make sure that he understands the extent of the work for which he will be quoting and taking responsibility.

In most cases you should be able to give your solicitor your letter and copies of the lists that you have made, and it should be possible for him to prepare a quote in the same meeting. On rare occasions it may be necessary to leave the papers with him. If this should be the case, you should set a definite and short time limit – e.g. say you need to pick up the papers later the same day.

Remember that you will have to work with your solicitor and possibly be in contact with him over a long period, so the exercise is not just about obtaining a quote for the work that is fair and reasonable – it is about determining whether you would feel comfortable working with the solicitor that you instruct. You should be conscious of the impression that your solicitor makes on you during your initial meeting. This might influence whether you instruct him, irrespective of the quote that you are given.

When you have obtained your quote, you should put the advice in Section 8 into effect and obtain more quotes.

(*See precedent letter 21 in Appendix 2.*)

9.2.2 How long will it take your solicitor to do the work?

In order to gauge how competitive the quotes are, it will help you if you know how long it will take your solicitor to do the work involved. Unfortunately there is no definite guide, as every estate is different. There are a number of observations that can be made, however.

If the estate is relatively simple, and you are taking Option 2, the documents that your solicitor will need to prepare for your application for probate should take less than an hour. He will then need to spend additional time performing the checks that you have requested (with a simple estate with few papers, this may only take a few minutes). And he will also need to see you to go through the documents he has prepared for you, and have you sign them. This is probably a 15-minute job.

In total, then, if you have a simple, straightforward estate, it should take your solicitor between one and two hours to do all the work that you have instructed him to quote for. So if your solicitor's charge-out rate is usually £180 per hour plus VAT, it would be reasonable to expect a quote of between £180 and £360 plus VAT to obtain probate and advise you.

Appendix 1, Tables 3 and 4 illustrate what is involved in obtaining probate for a simple, straightforward estate.

Table 5 in Appendix 2 may help you to make sense of the quotes that you receive – but the information it contains should not be used in isolation. Consider it in conjunction with the other information given in this book and as no more than a very rough guide.

9.2.3 Good quote, bad quote reprise

How much should your solicitor quote for obtaining probate? How much for obtaining probate and providing advice on the administration of the estate?

One guideline (which does not seem atypical) is the service offered by Bernard Chill & Axtell (www.bcasol.co.uk) who will obtain a grant of probate for a fixed fee of £350 + VAT, provided that the estate has a gross value of less than £312,000 and no advice is required.

The absolute low-cost benchmark for the cost of obtaining probate plus advice would appear to be, at the time of writing, the service offered by Probate UK (www.probateuk.info/fees.html) which is a trading name of Westmans Law. I emailed Probate UK and asked whether their fees were intended to cover only the cost of extracting a grant of probate, and was informed that their fees "include applying for the grant together with advising the pr [a 'pr' is a personal representative: the individual administering the estate; an executor if there is a will, or an administrator if there isn't] in regard to administering the estate until the estate is finally wound up."

As Westmans operates as a virtual law firm with no offices, it is unlikely that a high street firm would be able to compete with their fees. However, they provide at least a target to aim for. If you decide on the strength of this to instruct Probate UK, remember that this is not an endorsement!

Probate UK have a scale of fees. An example (taken from their website) is that for an estate of £50,000 to £500,000 they charge £1200 + VAT. You will need to visit their website to obtain full details of their scale of fees.

There are various qualifications and caveats which you will need to check for yourself before you consider using them.

9.2.4 Possible difficulties/objections you may encounter

I have noticed one firm (which shall remain nameless) advertising on the internet, which states on its website that there is no point in obtaining asset valuations yourself as this will not save on fees. This (it is argued) is because you will neglect to obtain information about income tax etc, which will mean that the solicitors have to write again on your behalf. Hence duplication of work and no saving on their time in administering the estate.

Provided that you use the document pack provided in this book at Appendix 2, however, this problem will not arise and the criticism cannot be levelled. The valuation letters in the document pack request all the information that solicitors normally ask for at the outset of a probate matter.

You may find that some firms of solicitors argue that there would be no saving in time if you do part of the work because they would have to check all your work prior to signing off the estate. This is probably little more than an excuse to maintain high charges. The reality is that it all depends on what work you ask them to do and what the retainer is for.

Moreover, in most cases checking what you have done (if this is really necessary) will take less time than doing the work from scratch. For example, if you have obtained valuations, then checking that you have listed all the assets and not omitted any, and that you have asked the correct questions in your valuation letters, will take far less time than making a list of the assets and sending letters out and checking the letters as they come in – particularly as any checking that is done will have to be done in real time, whereas letter writing would be done in solicitors' time (see Appendix 1 for an illustration of the distinction).

You may find that some solicitors are reluctant to work with you on the basis that you will do some of the work and they will do some of the work. The commercial reality is probably that if they will not accept such an arrangement, there are others who will, for a price. You just have to agree on a price which is competitive. Hopefully this book will have given you sufficient information to enable you to negotiate a competitive price.

9.2.5 Obtaining probate

When you have decided which solicitor to use, you should pass on your files of papers to enable him to prepare your application for probate. At the same time as you do this, you should provide him with a letter confirming the work agreed.

(*See precedent letter 22 in Appendix 2.*)

Your solicitor will send you his own client care letter for signature and return; you should read it carefully before you sign it.

9.3 Third Stage: Calling in the Assets

9.3.1 Introduction

Calling in the assets is time-consuming but usually not complicated. It is another area where a great deal of money in legal fees can be saved.

If you are carrying out any of this work, your solicitor should make sure that he gives you an adequate supply of copies of the probate to do the task. You will probably need a separate copy of the probate for each institution that you are dealing with.

You will need to write to the financial institutions involved and ask them to send you cheques for the money due. As you receive each cheque, it should be paid into your executorship bank account.

9.3.2 Bank and building society accounts and insurance policies

You will have a file of papers which will probably include withdrawal forms and encashment forms. You will simply need to complete the withdrawal forms and claim forms and post them with covering letters to the financial institutions. Some financial institutions will not have provided claim forms but instead will have said that they need a copy of the probate before they can proceed further.

(*See precedent letters 23 and 24 in Appendix 2.*)

9.3.3 Shares

If there are shares which are to be sold, you simply need to send these with a covering letter and copies of the probate to a stockbroker (bearing in mind any capital gains tax advice you may have received).

If the shares are to be transferred you may be able to transfer them yourself, but the fees charged by stockbrokers for this work are usually quite reasonable, so it might be advisable to have share transfers undertaken by a stockbroker to make sure that they are completed correctly.

(*See precedent letter 25 and 26 in Appendix 2.*)

9.3.4 Houses, flats and apartments

If there is a house or flat to be sold you will have been given a quote by your solicitor. You may choose to obtain a few quotes from licensed conveyancers before proceeding.

9.3.5 Pension/salary etc

You will need to fill in and return any documents you have received relating to pensions, and to write to claim any arrears of salary you have been informed about.

(*See precedent letters 27 and 28 in Appendix 2.*)

9.3.6 Complex financial instruments

Remember, a complex financial instrument for these purposes is any asset of any kind that you do not understand, and any trust.

These are best left to your solicitor to deal with.

9.4 Fourth Stage: Paying the Creditors

Once you have received money from the banks, building societies etc you can begin to pay the creditors. Remember to pay your solicitor promptly when you do!

This is another area where there are significant savings to be made, if you take care of it yourself rather than giving it to your solicitor to do. It is largely a matter of common sense – you simply pay money to the people and institutions owed. There are pitfalls, however.

If the estate is insolvent, you can easily come unstuck. If you have followed the advice given in this book, you will not be dealing with an insolvent estate – if the estate was insolvent, you would have given it to your solicitor.

Another pitfall is that, generally, it would be unwise to pay a mortgage debt from money received from a bank. Your initial letter of instruction should have prompted your solicitor to advise on this point in your particular case. If you have any doubts, ask him specifically about this issue.

(See precedent letter 29 in Appendix 2.)

9.4.1 Protection from creditors: a warning

If you are dealing with probate and you distribute the money from the estate without paying all the debts of the estate, you will have to approach the beneficiaries and request them to repay some of the money they have been given so that you can pay the creditors.

This will be embarrassing and unprofessional. Worse still, it could be expensive, because if you fail to get the money back from the beneficiaries, you may be held personally liable to pay the debts.

Where you have information that debts exist, there should be no problem with ensuring that you pay them (provided that your record keeping is effective). But what if there is a debt you do not know about, and which only comes to light after you have distributed the money?

You could remain liable for the debts and liabilities of the deceased after you have distributed assets to the beneficiaries, to the extent that there would have been assets available to pay those debts and liabilities had those assets not been distributed.

So even though you did not know about the debt, you may be held personally liable to pay for it.

There is a procedure, though, that you can follow to protect yourself from the prospect of being pursued by creditors in these circumstances. This consists of placing advertisements in certain newspapers giving notice that you are going to distribute the money from the estate. These advertisements should require anyone who is owed money to contact you giving details of their claim within a stated time, which must be at least two months from the date the advertisements appear. The advertisements should be in:

- the *London Gazette*

- if there is land to be distributed, a newspaper circulating in the district in which the land is situated (if there is no land to be distributed, this is not applicable)

- by "such other like notices, including notices elsewhere than in England and Wales, as would, in any special case, have been directed by a Court of competent jurisdiction in an action for administration."*

Normally an advertisement in the *London Gazette* and a newspaper local to where the deceased lived will suffice. If there is land owned by the deceased in an area away from where he lived, an advertisement should be placed in a newspaper covering that area.

For most cases you need do no more than that to protect yourself. It is usually possible to take a common sense view based on the background of the deceased and the constitution of his estate as to the advertisements required.

If you have doubts about your particular case, check with your solicitor that the advertisements you are placing will be adequate.

---

* In an administration action, a Court directs that advertisements should be placed in local or national newspapers that are appropriate to the case. If you are unable to determine what advertisements would satisfy this requirement, you can request a Court to certify the advertisements it would direct in an administration action.

The advertisements should be in a particular form. You can book the advertisement (known as an s27 Trustee Act advertisement) with the *London Gazette* by visiting their website. If you telephone a local newspaper, you should ask for a s27 Trustee Act advertisement, and be armed with details of the full name of the deceased, any alias he used, his date of death and the place of death.

Check the advertisements when they appear to make sure the information they contain is correct, and retain copies of the advertisements as evidence that you have placed them.

9.5 Fifth Stage: Preparing Estate Accounts/Begin Distributing the Estate

It is the usual practice to have a set of estate accounts prepared which are approved by the residuary beneficiaries before the residuary beneficiaries are paid.

As this book is about delegating all tasks that go beyond routine administration, you are recommended to delegate the task to a solicitor or an accountant. If the estate is taxable, you should ensure that the accountant, if one is used, is a tax accountant with expertise in inheritance tax.

You are also recommended to obtain a number of quotes.

When you have had estate accounts prepared, you are ready to pay the beneficiaries and finish work on the estate – subject to the information given in Sections 9.6.1, 9.6.2, 9.6.3, 9.7.1 and 9.7.2.

If you want to do the estate accounts yourself there is no set legal format for them. However, an example of how accounts might be presented is given in Appendix 3 and could be adapted to most situations.

9.5.1 Paying the beneficiaries

Yet another stage where significant savings can be made – but there are pitfalls for the unwary.

9.5.2 Paying the beneficiaries: a warning

If you have decided that advertisements are necessary as described in the previous section, you need to wait for the two-month expiry date to pass before you pay any beneficiary. (There is even a case to be made that you should allow this period to pass before you pay any of the creditors.)

In addition, if you have reason to believe that there may be a claim against the estate (or probably even if you do not have any such reason) you need to wait for a period of six months from the issue of the probate before you pay any of the beneficiaries. The safety first approach is always to wait for a period of six months.

The reason for the delay is that a claim might be contemplated by someone who feels they have not received as much as they should have done from the estate. This could be, for example, a child of the deceased who has not been mentioned in his will, or the spouse or civil partner of the deceased, or anyone financially supported by the deceased at the date of his death. (This list of possible claimants may not be exhaustive.)

If a claim were to be made, and it was successful, the estate would have to pay it. If you had distributed the estate within six months of the issue of probate, you could be made personally liable to pay the claim. By waiting for six months you protect yourself by eliminating this area of potential liability.

Many people, including solicitors, often take the view that a six-month delay is unnecessary if they know the circumstances of the case. However, the only circumstances in which it is entirely safe to distribute money within the six-month period are probably those in which you are the sole beneficiary. In all other cases the six-month delay is to be recommended. However well you think you knew the deceased, you might be unaware of something obscure (e.g. the existence of a secret partner or child) which could lead to a successful claim. This does not necessarily mean that no part of the estate can ever be distributed at an early stage; there may be one or more items of limited value given by the will which could safely be handed to the recipients.

You could also discuss the background of the deceased with your solicitor, and he could furnish you with a comfort letter about the matter, indicating who (if anyone) might have a valid claim against the estate. If your solicitor wants to keep his indemnity insurance premiums at a reasonable level, however, he is unlikely to give you a *carte blanche* to distribute the estate before the six months have expired, and his advice is likely to be hedged with caution.

Nevertheless, you may take the view that your knowledge of the deceased and his family circumstances is such that, once your solicitor has indicated the risks, you can distribute the estate before the six months have passed with impunity. If you choose to observe the six-month limit (and this book recommends that you do) you will need to inform the beneficiaries of what you are proposing, preferably at an early stage.

(*See precedent letter 30 in Appendix 2.*)

9.5.3 Paying the beneficiaries – a further warning

There is scope for serious error and loss when you pay the beneficiaries, if you do not proceed with care. You could pay the wrong person; you could pay the right person the wrong amount; you could pay a bankrupt or a minor; or you could send a cheque to the wrong address.

It may transpire that there is insufficient money in the estate to pay the beneficiaries what they are due under the will, or you may pay some in full then have insufficient funds left for the remaining beneficiaries.

If you do not trust yourself to get these details right, or if you do not understand what is due to whom, the task of paying the beneficiaries should be delegated to your solicitor.

9.5.4 Pay the legatees

You would normally pay the specific gifts of property (specific legacies) and gifts of set sums of money (pecuniary legacies) first. You are advised to ensure before you do that you contact the beneficiaries concerned to make sure that they have not changed address. If you know the individuals you could personally hand them their cheques or items of property; if not, you could write to them. Obtain receipts for all your payments, whether made by cash or cheque, or specific items of property. Note that interest is payable on pecuniary legacies paid more than one year after the date of death.

Precedent letter 31 includes a receipt which you could adapt for use in connection with a specific item of property.

(*See precedent letter 31 in Appendix 2.*)

9.6 Final Stage: Winding up the Estate

9.6.1 Check addresses

You should now be ready to pay the residuary beneficiaries and conclude matters. As with the legatees, you would be advised to ensure before you do that you telephone or email them to make sure that they have not changed address and neglected to inform you.

9.6.2 Circulate the estate accounts

This means sending the accounts to the residuary beneficiaries and asking for their signature and return.

(*See precedent letter 31 in Appendix 2.*)

9.6.3 Pay the residuary beneficiaries

First, consider making bankruptcy searches (see 9.7.3). Second, ask your accountant to prepare a form R185 for each residuary beneficiary. If you know the residuary beneficiaries well, you could personally hand them their cheques; if not, you could write to them. It is always wise to obtain receipts for your payments.

(See precedent letter 31 in Appendix 2.)

9.7 Other Matters to Consider

9.7.1 Interim distributions

With some estates it may be advisable to make a payment before you have collected and cashed in all the assets. An example of this would be where there was a substantial sum of money in a bank account and a house in the estate. You might be able to collect the money from the bank account fairly quickly, but the house might remain unsold for a long time.

In these circumstances, you might make a distribution of some of the money from the bank account (retaining a sum to cover contingencies) and make a second and final distribution of money following the sale of the house.

If you have any doubts as to what would be a sensible amount to distribute, you should discuss the matter with your solicitor.

9.7.2 Complex estates

Remember that some estates are complex and if the indications are that the one you are dealing with is one of them, you may need to discuss every stage with your solicitor or leave some aspects of the probate (such as distributions of money) in his hands.

If you opt for a situation where you instruct your solicitor to obtain probate and have further meetings with him to obtain written advice prior to taking the steps following probate, make sure that you and your solicitor both understand what advice is to be given, where his responsibilities end and yours begin, and what the basis of charging will be for the meetings and advice.

9.7.3 Bankrupt and minor beneficiaries

Do not make payments to bankrupt beneficiaries; and do not make payments to beneficiaries who are minors (i.e. under the age of 18) without first taking legal advice. It could prove costly to you personally even though you are acting as an executor or administrator.

9.7.4 Income tax after the date of death

Income received on the estate assets after the date of death is taxed at the basic rate. There is no personal allowance that would make some of the income tax-free.

The executors/administrators (i.e. you) are responsible for paying the tax due on this income.

Usually this is not an issue, as the income in most cases will be taxed at source. However, when untaxed income is received it is an issue. You must either ensure that your advisor accounts to HMRC for the tax in a timely manner to avoid penalties or do it yourself if you consider yourself competent.

9.7.5 Final words of advice

You may be held personally liable for your errors, so consider and protect against the downside at all times. And consider the need to retain your file of papers for 12 years or more after you have finished.

10. Saving Money if You Choose Option 3

Doing Everything Yourself

If you are interested in doing everything yourself, you could begin by obtaining three official forms – IHT205 and IHT206, and PA1. These should all be available from your local probate registry and from the internet at www.hmrc.gov.uk and www.hmcourts-service.gov.uk/infoabout/civil/probate/index.htm.

If you are confident that you understand these forms, and that the estate is a low value or exempt estate as defined by HMRC in forms IHT205 and IHT206, then you may be able to proceed with administering the estate by yourself (subject to understanding the will, etc).

Even if the estate is a higher value estate and/or has issues requiring the completion of an IHT400 form, you may be able to successfully complete it and administer the estate without assistance. However, bear in mind the extent to which you are potentially exposing yourself to loss, and the fact that you are on your own.

A brief explanation of the forms may be helpful.

- Form PA1 is used to determine who you are and whether you are entitled to obtain Probate. It contains guidance notes and there is an accompanying form – PA1a – giving further guidance. Provided you follow all the guidance notes you probably cannot go far wrong with form PA1.

- Form IHT 205 is used to provide details of low-value or exempt estates, and form IHT 206 gives guidance on how to fill it in correctly. Provided you follow the guidance notes on the form itself and in IHT 206, and understand the guidance given, completing the form should not be a problem for most people.

- Form IHT 400 is used to provide details of higher-value estates, usually those with inheritance tax implications. The 81-page booklet 'IHT400 Notes' contains extensive guidance on completing the form. Again, provided you understand the guidance and follow it all, you should be able to complete the form.

However, some may not find understanding the guidance for IHT 205 or IHT 400 straightforward, and as a risk limitation exercise it may be advisable to instruct a solicitor, particularly if you have any doubts whatsoever about your level of understanding.

This book does not provide guidance on filling in the forms as the official guidance given would be difficult to improve upon.

If you go down this route, it is suggested that you acquaint yourself with inheritance tax, possibly starting with the guidance available at www.willsprobateandmore.co.uk.

It will help you if you read through the step-by-step instructions given in Section 9. Remember, if you go down this route, you are on your own trusting your own judgement and must bear any and all risks yourself without the protection of a solicitor's advice and indemnity insurance.

It is acknowledged that the estate that you are administering may be suitable for you to deal with entirely on your own using only the contents of this book (or the contents of this book and other reference material); and that you may be personally competent to deal with it. But in view of the risks, it cannot be recommended.

If you are applying for probate yourself you should follow the procedures given in section 9.1, then instead of instructing a solicitor as advised in section 9.2, you should fill in the forms appropriate to your probate matter and deal with them as instructed in the explanatory notes which accompany the forms. You will in due course receive probate from the Probate Registry. When this happens, you will be able to implement the steps given in 9.3 to 9.6 (or such of those steps as you feel competent to undertake).

Appendices

Appendix 1

How to Estimate the Time it Will Take Your Solicitor to do the Work That You Instruct Him to Do

Note

These are estimates of time taken for various tasks your solicitor does in probate. They are based on the author's own experience. They will not apply to every solicitor or to every situation.

It is not my intention to imply that your particular matter will not take a great deal of your solicitor's time, or that there are strict rules that can be applied to every case. At best these are guidelines which will help in many matters (possibly most) to estimate the approximate time it will take to carry out a probate from start to finish.

In addition, bear in mind that although your solicitor may not need to spend a great deal of his own time on your matter, this does not necessarily mean that your matter will be concluded quickly. Probate is notorious for taking a long time. Often there is (for instance) a house that needs to be sold to conclude matters, and the sale of the house proves problematical.

Table 1: Straightforward probate, Option 1 – 'solicitors' time'

This table provides an estimate of the time it will take your solicitor to deal with probate for a very simple, straightforward estate – e.g. one consisting of four bank accounts and three insurance policies, and with three creditors, three beneficiaries, and a straightforward will naming one executor, and no inheritance tax implications. It is assumed that you are giving the solicitor the entire probate, as per Option 1.

All tasks are given in 'solicitors' time', that is, time in units of six minutes.

Task Performed by Solicitor	Estimate of Time it Should Take
Receive your letter instructing him that you accept his quote	6 min
Open file	6 min (mostly done by secretary)
Send you a client care letter	6 min
Receive your signed client care letter	6 min
Initial meeting with you to receive papers and to obtain evidence of your identity	30 min
Peruse papers	18 min
Read will and note contents	18 min
Write valuation letters	42 min
Write to creditors	18 min
Receive valuation letters	42 min
Receive letters from creditors	18 min
Receive sundry correspondence	12 min
Prepare withdrawal forms/claim forms	12 min

Task Performed by Solicitor	Estimate of Time it Should Take
Prepare IHT205(2006) (one of the probate documents)	18 min (the work mainly involves filling in the blanks in a precedent form – the form automatically adds up the figures inserted in it, sparing the solicitor this task)
Prepare oath (the other probate document)	18 min (the work mainly involves filling in the blanks in a precedent form)
Check/proofread work	12 min
Letter confirming advice given during initial meeting and asking you to visit to sign oath and IHT205	18 min
Second meeting with you to go through oath and IHT205	18 min
Letter to probate registry	6 min
Probate received from probate registry	6 min
Letters sending probate to banks etc	42 min
Payments received from banks etc	42 min
Payments made to creditors	18 min
Letters acknowledging payment received from creditors	18 min
Preparing estate accounts	24 min
Circulating estate accounts	18 min
Receiving signed estate accounts	18 min
Preparing forms R185	18 min
Paying beneficiaries	18 min
Receiving receipts from beneficiaries	18 min
Preparation/perusal/thinking time throughout	36 min
Letter to you confirming estate wound up	12 min
Total Time Taken	10 hours 12 min

Table 2: Straightforward probate, Option 1 – real time

This table provides an estimate of the time it will take your solicitor to deal with probate for the same estate shown in Table 1, in the same circumstances. However, in this table all tasks are given in real time – i.e. the length of time that, realistically, they actually take.

Task Performed by Solicitor	Estimate of Time it Should Take
Receive your letter instructing him you accept his quote	1 min
Open file	1 min (mostly done by secretary)
Send you a client care letter	1 min (standard letter)
Receive your signed client care letter	1 min
Initial meeting with you to receive papers and to obtain evidence of your identity	25 min
Peruse papers	12.5 min
Read will and note contents	12.5 min
Write valuation letters	8 min (using standard letters – as per Appendix 2)
Write to creditors	3 min (using standard letters – as per Appendix 2)
Receive valuation letters	8 min
Receive letters from creditors	3 min
Receive sundry correspondence	2 min
Prepare withdrawal forms/claim forms	8 min

Task Performed by Solicitor	Estimate of Time it Should Take
Prepare IHT205(2006) (one of the probate documents)	14 min (the work mainly involves filling in the blanks in a precedent form – the form automatically adds up the figures inserted in it, sparing the solicitor this task)
Prepare oath (the other probate document)	14 min (the work mainly involves filling in the blanks in a precedent form)
Check/proofread work	8 min
Letter confirming advice given during initial meeting and asking you to visit to sign oath and IHT205	12.5 min
Second meeting with you to go through oath and IHT205	15 min
Letter to probate registry	1 min
Probate received from probate registry	1 min
Letters sending probate to banks etc	7 min
Payments received from banks etc	7 min
Payments made to creditors	3 min
Letters acknowledging payment received from creditors	3 min
Preparing estate accounts	20 min
Circulating estate accounts	3 min
Receiving signed estate accounts	3 min
Preparing forms R185	15 min
Paying beneficiaries	3 min
Receiving receipts from beneficiaries	3 min
Preparation/perusal/thinking time throughout	31 min
Letter to you confirming estate wound up	6.5 min
Total Time Taken	4 hours 16 min

Table 3: Straightforward probate, Option 2 – 'solicitors' time'

This table provides an estimate of the time it will take your solicitor to deal with an application for probate for the same very simple, straightforward estate described at the head of Table 1 – an estate consisting of four bank accounts and three insurance policies and with three beneficiaries, a straightforward will naming one executor, and with no inheritance tax implications (it is assumed that you have done the stage 1 work yourself and have instructed your solicitor as per the advice in this book).

All tasks are given in 'solicitors' time', that is, time in units of six minutes.

Task Performed by Solicitor	Estimate of Time it Should Take
Receive your letter instructing him you accept his quote	6 min
Open file	6 min (mostly done by secretary)
Send you a client care letter	6 min
Receive your signed client care letter	6 min
Initial meeting with you to receive papers and to give verbal advice etc as requested in your instructions	30 min
Peruse papers	12 min
Read will and note contents	18 min
Check your lists	6 min

Task Performed by Solicitor	Estimate of Time it Should Take
Prepare IHT205(2006) (one of the probate documents)	18 min (the work mainly involves filling in the blanks in a precedent form – the form automatically adds up the figures inserted in it, sparing the solicitor this task)
Prepare oath (the other probate document)	18 min (the work mainly involves filling in the blanks in a precedent form)
Check/proofread work	12 min
Letter confirming advice given during initial meeting and asking you to visit to sign oath and IHT205	18 min
Second meeting with you to go through oath and IHT205	18 min
Letter to probate registry	6 min
Letter received from probate registry	6 min
Letter to you enclosing probate and his bill	6 min
Total Time Taken	3 hours 12 min

Table 4: Straightforward probate, Option 2 – real time

This table provides an estimate of the time it will take your solicitor to deal with the same work as per Table 3. However, in this table all tasks are given in real time – i.e. the length of time that they probably actually take.

Task Performed by Solicitor	Estimate of Time it Should Take
Receive your letter instructing him you accept his quote	1 min
Open file	1 min (mostly done by secretary)
Send you a client care letter	1 min
Receive your signed client care letter	1 min
Initial meeting with you to receive papers and to give verbal advice etc as requested in your instructions	25 min
Peruse papers	7 min
Read will and note contents	12.5 min
Check your lists	5 min
Prepare IHT205(2006) (one of the probate documents)	14 min (the work mainly involves filling in the blanks in a precedent form – the form automatically adds up the figures inserted in it, sparing the solicitor this task)
Prepare oath (the other probate document)	14 min (the work mainly involves filling in the blanks in a precedent form)

Task Performed by Solicitor	Estimate of Time it Should Take
Check/proofread work	8 min
Letter confirming advice given during initial meeting and asking you to visit to sign oath and IHT205	12.5 min
Second meeting with you to go through oath and IHT205	15 min
Letter to probate registry	1 min
Letter received from probate registry	1 min
Letter to you enclosing probate and his bill	1 min
Total Time Taken	2 hours

Table 5: Probate time calculator

This is a tool which may enable you to very roughly estimate how long it will take your solicitor to carry out the work that you instruct him to do. Note that it is a blunt instrument and should not be taken as an absolute guide. It may help you to gauge whether a quote that you have received is competitive, when considered in conjunction with the other advice and information given in this book.

Bear in mind that you may not even need to refer to it, given the other information provided to help you to gauge whether the quotes you receive are competitive.

You will need to factor into your calculations the time that your solicitor may spend on receiving sundry correspondence (e.g. statements from utility companies) and on writing to you with progress reports or holding meetings with you.

Task	Description of Work Involved	'Solicitors' Time'	Real (Actual) Time
Initial meeting with you to discuss the matter – simple estate	Obtaining information from you and evidence of your identity, and discussing the contents of the will or distribution of the estate under the rules of intestacy	30 mins	30 mins
Initial meeting with you to discuss the matter – complex estate	Obtaining information from you and evidence of your identity, and discussing the contents of the will or distribution of the estate under the rules of intestacy	90 mins	90 mins
Perusing papers at the outset of the matter (other than the will)	This will involve looking at all bank account details, insurance policies, bills etc and making lists of each	35 sec to review and list each document, rounded up to nearest 6 mins. E.g. 50 documents = 30 mins	35 sec to review and list each document. E.g. 50 documents = 29 mins
Perusing a simple will	Reading the will and noting and writing down the contents	12 mins	8 mins

Task	Description of Work Involved	'Solicitors' Time'	Real (Actual) Time
Perusing a complex will	Reading the will and noting and writing down the contents	24 mins	20 mins
Client care letter	Writing to you with contractual terms of engagement	6 min	1 min
Dealing with a bank account (note that this illustrates why it is a good idea to do your own valuations and cash-in the assets yourself – if it is safe to do so)	Sending a letter to value the account, receiving a valuation, preparing a withdrawal form, sending the form plus probate to the bank and receiving the money	4 letters at 6 min each plus withdrawal form at 6 min. Total: 30 min	4 letters at 1 min each plus withdrawal form at 1 min. Total: 5 min
Dealing with an insurance policy (note that this illustrates why it is a good idea to do your own valuations and cash in the assets yourself – if it is safe to do so)	Sending a letter to value the policy, receiving a valuation, preparing a claim form, sending the form plus probate to the insurance company and receiving the money	4 letters at 6 min each plus claim form at 6 min. Total: 30 min	4 letters at 1 min each plus claim form at 1 min. Total: 5 min

Task	Description of Work Involved	'Solicitors' Time'	Real (Actual) Time
Dealing with a shareholding (note that this illustrates why it is a good idea to do your own valuations and cash in the assets yourself – if it is safe to do so)	Sending letter to registrars, receiving letter from registrars, sending probate etc to stockbrokers, receiving sale form from stockbrokers, sending sale form to stockbrokers, receiving cheque from stockbrokers	6 letters at 6 min each. Total: 36 min	6 letters at 1 min each. Total: 6 min
Preparing papers to lead to obtain probate for a small straightforward estate (e.g. a few bank accounts, a house, shares, and no complex issues)	Preparing oath. Preparing form IHT205 (2006)	Oath: 18 min. IHT205: 18 min. Total: 36 min.	Oath: 14 min. IHT205: 14 min. Total: 28 min.
Preparing papers to lead to obtain probate for a small estate with modest issues (e.g. a few bank accounts, a house, shares, no will, deceased divorced, and minor beneficiaries)	Preparing oath. Preparing form IHT205 (2006).	Oath: 42 min. IHT205: 18 min. Total: 58 min	Oath: 40 min. IHT205: 14 min. Total: 54 min.

Task	Description of Work Involved	'Solicitors' Time'	Real (Actual) Time
Preparing papers to lead to obtain probate for a large estate with no complex issues, no lifetime gifts	Preparing oath. Preparing form IHT400. Form IHT depends on the number of assets, but assuming 10 straightforward assets at 8 min per asset, 10 min for information about deceased, and 30 min for checking/calculating IHT.	Oath: 18 min. Preparing form IHT400: 120 min. Total: 138 min	Oath: 14 min. Preparing form IHT400: 120 min. Total: 134 min.
Preparing papers to lead to obtain probate for a large estate with straightforward lifetime gifts	Preparing oath. Preparing form IHT400. Form IHT depends on the number of assets and complexity but assuming 10 straightforward assets at 8 min per asset, 10 min for information about deceased, four lifetime gifts at 10 min to consider each and 30 min for checking/calculating IHT.	Oath: 18 min. Preparing form IHT400: 162 min. Total: 180 min	Oath: 18 min. Preparing form IHT400: 160 min. Total: 178 min
Preparing papers to lead to obtain probate for a large estate with some complexities	Preparing oath. Preparing form IHT400. Form IHT depends on the number of assets and complexity but assuming 10 straightforward assets at 8 min per asset, private company shares with partial BPR at 30 min, 10 min for information about deceased, four lifetime gifts at 15 min to consider each and 50 min for checking/calculating IHT.	Oath: 42 min. Preparing form IHT400: 234 min. Total: 276 min	Oath: 40 min. Preparing form IHT400: 230 min. Total: 270 min

Task	Description of Work Involved	'Solicitors' Time'	Real (Actual) Time
Second meeting with you to sign probate papers – simple estate	Reading through oath and IHT205 and agreeing contents	18 min	15 min
Second meeting with you to sign probate papers – complex estate	Reading through oath and IHT400 and agreeing contents	60 min (could be less or more)	60 min (could be less or more)
Preparing deed for use with nil-rate band will trust (to transfer entire trust fund to surviving spouse or civil partner)	Reading through will, considering instructions and drafting and proofreading deed (usually a precedent will be used, which only involves adding name and address details – but getting the right precedent is critical)	Deed: 60 min (could be less)	Deed: 55 min (could be less)
Preparing deed for use with nil-rate band will trust (to create a loan to surviving spouse – may be appropriate in a care fees situation)	Reading through will, considering instructions and drafting and proofreading deed (usually a precedent will be used, which only involves adding name and address details – but getting the right precedent is critical)	Deed: 90 min (could be less)	Deed: 85 min (could be less)
Deed of variation, to transfer a pecuniary legacy from one person to another	Reading through will, considering instructions and drafting and proofreading deed (usually a precedent will be used, which only involves adding name and address details)	Deed: 36 min (could be less)	Deed: 32 min (could be less)

Task	Description of Work Involved	'Solicitors' Time'	Real (Actual) Time
Deed of variation, to transfer a share of residue from one person to another	Reading through will, considering instructions and drafting and proofreading deed (usually a precedent will be used, which only involves adding name and address details)	Deed: 60 min (could be less)	Deed: 55 min (could be less)
Deed of variation, incorporating a new will	Reading through will, considering instructions and drafting and proofreading deed (much depends on the new will; could be a precedent, which only involves adding name and address details, or could be custom drafted)	If precedent can be used: 60 min. If custom-drafted: 120 min (could be less)	If precedent can be used: 55 min. If custom-drafted: 120 min (could be less)
Preparing estate accounts for straightforward and simple estate	Going through ledger card and correspondence, drawing up accounts and balancing against figures in ledger	If done manually: 30 min – 1 hour. If case management used: may be possible to produce in minutes	If done manually: 30 min – 1 hour. If case management used: may be possible to produce in minutes

Task	Description of Work Involved	'Solicitors' Time'	Real (Actual) Time
Preparing estate accounts for a large estate	Going through ledger card and correspondence, drawing up accounts and balancing against figures in ledger	If done manually: depends on estate – could be 2-4 hours or more. If case management used: may be possible to produce in minutes	If done manually: depends on estate – could be 2-4 hours or more. If case management used: may be possible to produce in minutes
Paying a beneficiary (note that this illustrates why it is a good idea to pay the beneficiaries yourself – if it is safe to do so)	Writing to beneficiary, receiving ID, sending estate accounts, receiving estate accounts, sending cheque and obtaining receipt	6 letters at 6 mins each. Total: 36 mins	6 letters at 1 min each. Total: 6 mins

Appendix 2

Bank of Precedent Letters

Note

The precedent letters contain square brackets. Sometimes these are used to indicate that you need to insert information such as the name and address of the deceased. At other times they are used to indicate that you have to choose between two phrases, depending on the circumstances.

The letters to the beneficiaries have been drafted on the basis that the beneficiaries are unknown to you; you may have to adapt them depending on your knowledge of the individuals concerned.

The letters should cover all the situations that you will encounter with most estates. If there is a circumstance not covered by these letters, they should assist you in composing an appropriate letter yourself.

Precedent letter 1 – to bank/building society to pay funeral bill

[Insert named and address of bank/building society]

[Insert your own name and address]

[Date]

Dear Sirs,

The late [insert name of deceased]

Account number(s) [insert account details]

I am writing to inform you that the above named account holder has recently died. I enclose a registrar's copy of the death certificate together with a copy of the funeral bill for your reference.

I am the personal representative dealing with the estate.

I would be grateful if you would send a cheque to the funeral director to pay the funeral bill as soon as reasonably possible, and write to me to confirm that this has been done.

Thank you for your assistance.

Yours faithfully,

....[signature]

N.B. Remember to enclose the death certificate and a copy of the funeral bill.

Precedent letter 2 – to solicitors to obtain the will

[Insert named and address of solicitors]

[Insert your own name and address]

[Date]

Dear Sirs,

The late [insert name of deceased]

I am writing to inform you that the above named client has recently died. I enclose a registrar's copy of the death certificate for your reference.

I am the execut[or / rix] named in the will.

[I will visit to collect the will so please ensure it is made available and placed on reception for me within the next 48 hours. / Please send the original will to my home address by registered post as soon as possible.]

Yours faithfully,

....[signature]

N.B. Remember to enclose the death certificate.

Precedent letter 3 – valuation letter to IFA / accountant / stockbroker etc

[Insert named and address of IFA/accountant/stockbroker]

[Insert your own name and address]

[Date]

Dear Sirs,

The late [Insert name of deceased] of [insert address]

I am writing to inform you that the above named client has recently died. I enclose a registrar's copy of the death certificate for your reference.

I am the personal representative dealing with the estate.

I would be grateful if you would check your records and provide me with details of any investments held in the name of the deceased. When you do so, please give me detailed values of the investments at the date of death, including (if applicable) interest accrued but not credited.

If applicable, please let me have details of the interest paid to the deceased during the last financial year from April 6 to the date of death, including figures for the income tax paid and the net interest/income of the deceased during the period.

Additional/alternative paragraphs for accountants only where the deceased held business or agricultural property:

I understand that the late [name of deceased] owned [shares in . . . . . Ltd] [an interest in the . . . . . Partnership] [the farm known as . . . . .] [and I understand that you prepared the annual accounts]. I require a valuation at the date of death for the purposes of probate and inheritance tax, with information about whether and to what extent [business property relief] [agricultural property relief] would be available.

[Please provide details of your proposed fess for providing a valuation.]

Thank you for your assistance.

Yours faithfully,

....[signature]

N.B. Remember to enclose the death certificate and a copy of the funeral bill.

Precedent letter 4 – valuation letter to bank/building society

[Insert name and address of bank/building society]

[Insert your own name and address]

[Date]

Dear Sirs,

The late [insert name of deceased] of [insert address]

Account number(s) [insert account details]

I am writing to inform you that the above named account holder has recently died. I enclose a registrar's copy of the death certificate for your reference.

I am the personal representative dealing with the estate.

I would be grateful if you would provide me with:

- details of the balance(s) in the above numbered account(s) at the date of death, including interest accrued but not credited
- the same information for any other accounts held by the deceased
- details of the interest paid to the deceased during the last financial year from April 6 to the date of death, including figures for income tax paid and the net interest paid during the period
- details of any items stored in safe custody on behalf of the deceased; and
- withdrawal forms to close the numbered accounts held in the name of the deceased.

Thank you for your assistance.

Yours faithfully,

....[signature]

N.B. Remember to enclose the death certificate.

Precedent letter 5 – valuation letter to insurance company

[Insert name and address of insurance company]

[Insert your own name and address]

[Date]

Dear Sirs,

The late [insert name of deceased] of [insert address]

Policy number(s) [insert policy details]

I am writing to inform you that the above named policyholder has recently died. I enclose a registrar's copy of the death certificate for your reference.

I am the personal representative dealing with the estate.

I would be grateful if you would provide me with:

- details of the value(s) of the above numbered polic[y / ies] at the date of death
- the same information for any other policies held by the deceased
- details of whether you are aware that [the policy is / any of the policies are] subject to trusts of any kind
- claim forms to cash and policy held in the name of the deceased.

Thank you for your assistance.

Yours faithfully,

....[signature]

N.B. Remember to enclose the death certificate.

Precedent letter 6 – letter to registrars confirming shareholding

[Insert named and address of registrars]

[Insert your own name and address]

[Date]

Dear Sirs,

The late [insert name of deceased] of [insert address]

[Insert name of company] plc

I am writing to inform you that the above named shareholder has recently died. I enclose a registrar's copy of the death certificate for your reference, together with the original share certificate(s).

I am the personal representative dealing with the estate.

I would be grateful if you would note the death in your records and return the share certificate to me, together with the death certificate, and confirm the number of shares held in the name of the deceased.

Thank you for your assistance.

Yours faithfully,

....[signature]

N.B. Remember to enclose the death certificate and share certificate(s), and to retain a copy of the share certificate(s) on your file.

Precedent letter 7 – letter to stockbrokers requesting valuation

[Insert named and address of stockbrokers]

[Insert your own name and address]

[Date]

Dear Sirs,

The late [insert name of deceased]

Further to our recent telephone conversation, I am writing to request a valuation for probate purposes of the shares held in the name of the late [insert name of deceased].

The shareholdings are as follows:

Company	Number and type of shares
[Insert name of company]	[Insert share details of each company, e.g. 500 10p ordinary shares]

I enclose a copy of the death certificate for your reference.

I look forward to hearing from you in the near future.

Thank you for your assistance.

Yours faithfully,

....[signature]

N.B. Remember to enclose the death certificate.

Precedent letter 8 – letter to stockbrokers requesting valuation and confirmation of shareholding

[Insert named and address of stockbrokers]

[Insert your own name and address]

[Date]

Dear Sirs,

The late [insert name of deceased]

Further to our recent telephone conversation, I am writing to request a valuation for probate purposes of the shares held in the name of the late [insert name of deceased]. In addition, I would be grateful if you would notify the share registrars of the death and confirm the shareholdings for me.

I enclose a registrar's copy of the death certificate for your reference, together with the original share certificate(s).

I look forward to hearing from you in the near future.

Thank you for your assistance.

Yours faithfully,

....[signature]

N.B. Remember to enclose the death certificate and share certificate(s), and to retain a copy of the share certificate(s) on your file.

Precedent letter 9 – valuation letter for DWP state pension

[Insert DWP address details]

[Insert your own name and address]

[Date]

Dear Sirs,

The late [insert name of deceased] of [insert address]

National Insurance no: [insert NI number]

I am writing to inform you that the above named pensioner has recently died. I enclose a registrar's copy of the death certificate for your reference.

I am the personal representative dealing with the estate.

I would be grateful if you would provide me with details of any arrears of pension owing to the deceased, or of any refund due to the DWP if an overpayment has been made.

Thank you for your assistance.

Yours faithfully,

....[signature]

N.B. Remember to enclose the death certificate.

Precedent letter 10 – valuation letter for company pension

[Insert name and address of company pension trustees]

[Insert your own name and address]

[Date]

Dear Sirs,

The late [insert name of deceased] of [insert address]

National Insurance no: [insert NI number]

Work pension reference: [insert other references used by pension company or trustees]

I am writing to inform you that the above named pension scheme member has recently died. I enclose a registrar's copy of the death certificate for your reference.

I am the personal representative dealing with the estate.

I would be grateful if you would provide me with:

- details of any arrears of pension owing to the deceased, or of any refund due to the pension fund if an overpayment has been made
- details of any lump sum payments or any other payments such as a widow's pension due as a result of the death of the pensioner
- details of any nomination made by the pensioner
- details of the pension paid to the deceased during the last financial year from April 6 to the date of death, including figures for income tax paid and the net pension of the deceased during the period.

Thank you for your assistance.

Yours faithfully,

....[signature]

N.B. Remember to enclose the death certificate.

Precedent letter 11 – valuation letter for personal pension policy (pension not taken)

[Insert name and address of insurance company]

[Insert your own name and address]

[Date]

Dear Sirs,

The late [insert name of deceased] of [insert address]

National Insurance no: [insert NI number]

Pension plan number: [pension plan/policy no]

I am writing to inform you that the above named policyholder has recently died. I enclose a registrar's copy of the death certificate for your reference.

I am the personal representative dealing with the estate.

I would be grateful if you would provide me with:

• details of any lump sum payments or any other payments due to the estate as a result of the death of the pensioner

• details of any nomination made by the pensioner.

Thank you for your assistance.

Yours faithfully,

....[signature]

N.B. Remember to enclose the death certificate.

Precedent letter 12 – valuation letter for annuity

[Insert name and address of annuity co.]

[Insert your own name and address]

[Date]

Dear Sirs,

The late [insert name of deceased] of [insert address]

National Insurance no: [insert NI number]

Pension/annuity plan number: [insert pension/annuity plan no]

I am writing to inform you that the above named policyholder has recently died. I enclose a registrar's copy of the death certificate for your reference.

I am the personal representative dealing with the estate.

I would be grateful if you would provide me with:

- details of any arrears of pension owing to the deceased, or of any refund due to the pension fund if an overpayment has been made

- details of any payments such as a widow's pension due as a result of the death of the pensioner

- details of the pension paid to the deceased during the last financial year from April 6 to the date of death, including figures for income tax paid and the net pension of the deceased during the period.

Thank you for your assistance.

Yours faithfully,

....[signature]

N.B. Remember to enclose the death certificate.

Precedent letter 13 – valuation letter for wages/salary

[Insert name and address of employer]

[Insert your own name and address]

[Date]

Dear Sirs,

The late [insert name of deceased] of [insert address]

National Insurance no: [insert NI number]

Payroll no: [insert payroll no]

I am writing to inform you that the above named employee has recently died. I enclose a registrar's copy of the death certificate for your reference.

I am the personal representative dealing with the estate.

I would be grateful if you would provide me with:

- details of any arrears of pay owing to the deceased

- a cheque payable to me in my capacity as personal representative if arrears of pay are owed to the estate

- details of the wages/salary paid to the deceased during the last financial year from April 6 to the date of death, including figures for income tax paid and the net pay of the deceased during the period.

Thank you for your assistance.

Yours faithfully,

....[signature]

N.B. Remember to enclose the death certificate.

Precedent letter 14 – letter to utility company

[Insert name and address of gas/water/electricity company]

[Insert your own name and address]

[Date]

Dear Sirs,

The late [insert name of deceased] of [insert address]

Customer ref no: [insert reference number from bill]

I am writing to inform you that the above named customer has recently died. I enclose a Registrar's copy of the death certificate for your reference.

[The current meter reading is ....]

I am the personal representative dealing with the estate.

I would be grateful if you would provide me with an up-to-date statement, and a refund if any refund is due on the account.

Please send the statement, the refund (if applicable) and all other correspondence to me for my attention at the above address until further notice.

Please note that if the estate owes money on the account, it may not be possible to pay the money owed until after the issue of probate. At present it is not known when that will be.

Thank you for your assistance.

Yours faithfully,

....[signature]

N.B. Remember to enclose the death certificate.

Precedent letter 15 – letter to credit card company

[Insert name of bank/credit card company]

[Insert your own name and address]

[Date]

Dear Sirs,

The late [insert name of deceased] of [insert address]

Account no: [insert account no from statement]

I am writing to inform you that the above named customer has recently died. I enclose a registrar's copy of the death certificate for your reference.

I am the personal representative dealing with the estate.

I would be grateful if you would provide me with an up-to-date statement, and a refund if any refund is due on the account.

Please send the statement, the refund (if applicable) and all other correspondence to me for my attention at the above address until further notice.

Please note that if the estate owes money on the account, it may not be possible to pay the money owed until after the issue of probate. At present it is not known when that will be.

Thank you for your assistance.

Yours faithfully,

....[signature]

N.B. Remember to enclose the death certificate.

Precedent letter 16 – general letter to creditors

[Insert name of creditor/company owed money]

[Insert your own name and address]

[Date]

Dear Sirs,

The late [inert name of deceased] of [insert address]

[Insert details of debt and/or account no if applicable]

I am writing to inform you that the above named customer has recently died. I enclose a registrar's copy of the death certificate for your reference.

I am the personal representative dealing with the estate.

[I would be grateful if you would provide me with an up-to-date statement, and a refund if any refund is due on the account.]

Please send [the statement, the refund (if applicable) and] all [other] correspondence to me for my attention at the above address until further notice.

Please note that if the estate owes money [on the account], it may not be possible to pay the money owed until after the issue of probate. At present it is not known when that will be.

Thank you for your assistance.

Yours faithfully,

....[signature]

N.B. Remember to enclose the death certificate.

Precedent letter 17 – letter to beneficiary due to receive a specific item of property from a will

[Insert name and address of beneficiary]

[Insert your own name and address]

[Date]

Dear [insert name of beneficiary]

The late [insert name of deceased] of [insert address]

I am writing to inform you that [insert name of deceased] passed away on [insert date of death]. I am sorry to give you this news.

I am the personal representative dealing with the estate. There is a will which states that you are to receive [insert item given by will]. [I will make arrangements to have it delivered to you as soon as reasonably possible.]* [Please contact me to arrange to collect it.]*

I will need to be certain that you are the beneficiary named in the will, and I would be grateful if you would assist by providing evidence of your identity.

I will require for this purpose a photocopy of your passport or driving licence, together with a photocopy of a utility bill, council tax bill or bank statement. The copies of both documents should be certified by a solicitor as true copies of the originals.**

[Please also let me have details of your telephone number and email address to assist me to keep in touch with you.]

Finally, if you move house before receiving what you are due from the estate, please let me have details of your new address as soon as possible.

Thank you for your assistance.

Yours sincerely,

....[signature]

*The rule with specific gifts is that the beneficiary pays for all costs of packaging, transport and insurance unless the will states otherwise. So if the will simply states (for example) "I give my guitar to Tom", then Tom should collect the guitar. If the will states (for example) "I give my guitar to Tom free of all costs" then as executor you could pay to have the guitar shipped to Tom.

** How far you go with obtaining evidence of identity depends on the circumstances. However, you are better off being safe than sorry.

Precedent letter 18 – letter to beneficiary due to receive a specific sum of money from a will

[Insert name and address of beneficiary]

[Insert your own name and address]

[Date]

Dear [insert name of beneficiary]

The late [insert name of deceased] of [insert address]

I am writing to inform you that [insert name of deceased] passed away on [insert date of death]. I am sorry to give you this news.

I am the personal representative dealing with the estate. There is a will which states that you are to receive the sum of £[insert sum of money given by will]. Unfortunately, I am at an early stage in the administration of the estate and I do not as yet know how long it will be before I am able to pay the money due to you.

I will need to be certain before I pay you the money that you are the beneficiary named in the will, and I would be grateful if you would assist by providing evidence of your identity.

I will require for this purpose a photocopy of your passport or driving licence, together with a photocopy of a utility bill, council tax bill or bank statement. The copies of both documents should be certified by a solicitor as true copies of the originals.*

[Please let me have details of your telephone number and email address to assist me to keep in touch with you.]

Finally, if you move house before receiving what you are due from the estate, please let me have details of your new address as soon as possible.

Thank you for your assistance.

Yours sincerely,

....[signature]

* How far you go with obtaining evidence of identity depends on the circumstances. However, you are better off being safe than sorry.

Precedent letter 19 – letter to beneficiary due to receive a share of the residue under a will

[Insert name and address of beneficiary]

[Insert your own name and address]

[Date]

Dear [insert name of beneficiary]

The late [insert name of deceased] of [insert address]

I am writing to inform you that [insert name of deceased] passed away on [insert date of death]. I am sorry to give you this news.

I am the personal representative dealing with the estate.

There is a will which states that you are to receive a share of the residue of the estate. I enclose a copy for your reference.

Unfortunately, I am at an early stage in the administration of the estate and I do not as yet know how long it will be before I am able to pay the money due to you, nor do I know how much it will be.

I will need to be certain before I pay you the money that you are the beneficiary named in the will, and I would be grateful if you would assist by providing evidence of your identity.

I will require for this purpose a photocopy of your passport or driving licence, together with a photocopy of a utility bill, council tax bill or bank statement. The copies of both documents should be certified by a solicitor as true copies of the originals.*

[Please let me have details of your telephone number and email address to assist me to keep in touch with you.]

Finally, if you move house before receiving what you are due from the estate, please let me have details of your new address as soon as possible.

Thank you for your assistance.

Yours sincerely,

....[signature]

* How far you go with obtaining evidence of identity depends on the circumstances. However, you are better off being safe than sorry.

Precedent letter 20 – letter to beneficiary due to receive a share of the estate where there is no will

[Insert name and address of beneficiary]

[Insert your own name and address]

[Date]

Dear [insert name of beneficiary]

The late [insert name of deceased] of [insert address]

I am writing to inform you that [insert name of deceased] passed away on [insert date of death]. I am sorry to give you this news.

I am the personal representative dealing with the estate.

There is, as far as I know, no will, and this means that you are entitled to a share of the estate under the rules of intestacy.

Unfortunately, I am at an early stage in the administration of the estate and I do not as yet know how long it will be before I am able to pay the money due to you, nor do I know how much it will be.

I will need to be certain before I pay you the money that you are the beneficiary named in the will, and I would be grateful if you would assist by providing evidence of your identity.

I will require for this purpose a photocopy of your passport or driving licence, together with a photocopy of a utility bill, council tax bill or bank statement. The copies of both documents should be certified by a solicitor as true copies of the originals.*

Thank you for your assistance.

Yours sincerely,

....[signature]

* How far you go with obtaining evidence of identity depends on the circumstances. However, you are better off being safe than sorry.

Precedent letter 21 – letter to solicitors requesting quote

[Insert name and address of solicitors]

[Insert your own name and address]

[Date]

Dear Sirs,

The late [insert name of deceased] of [insert address]

Further to our recent meeting I enclose a list of assets and liabilities of the estate, together with a list of the beneficiaries indicating who they are and what they are due to receive from the estate. [I also enclose a copy of the will.]

You have seen the file of the papers belonging to the deceased, which formed the basis of my enquiries.

I would be grateful if you would give me a written quote for obtaining a grant of [probate / letters of administration] to the estate [and for dealing with any inheritance tax issues, including arranging payment of any inheritance tax that is due].

In addition please quote separately for [the conveyancing,] [any tax advice that might be appropriate,] [any work in relation to trusts,] [and for] carrying out the following:

[• looking through the papers of the deceased and checking them against my lists of assets and liabilities to make sure that the list is correct]

[• confirming that my list of assets correctly states whether the assets are the sole property of the deceased or jointly owned]

[• confirming that my list of beneficiaries is correct and that I have correctly stated what they should receive from the estate]

If you are planning on carrying out the third stage yourself...

[• providing written advice on whether any adverse consequences could arise from cashing in and transferring the assets and whether any action should be considered to mitigate capital gains tax before I proceed]

If you are planning on carrying out the fourth stage yourself...

[• providing written advice on whether I can safely pay all the debts from the money that I obtain from the banks etc]

[• providing written advice on whether a deed of variation or tax planning arrangement should be considered; and if so providing a quote for carrying out the deed of variation/tax planning]

[• providing written advice as to whether there are any issues not referred to above which could complicate administering the estate and paying the beneficiaries, such as lifetime trusts, conditional gifts or will trusts (if any) I have failed to consider (this is not intended as an exhaustive list of possible issues)]

[• providing a written explanation/advice on the following: [list any issues you fail to understand]]

[• advising me in writing of any enquiries I should make that I have not already made, e.g. for the purposes of completing the forms to obtain probate.]

As previously discussed, I require a fixed-fee quote, not an estimate.

Thank you for your assistance.

Yours faithfully,

....[signature]

Precedent letter 22 – letter to solicitors instructing them to act

Note

It is not intended that this entire letter should be used in all cases. You are encouraged to use only those paragraphs which apply to your circumstances. You may feel that you require advice at every stage and therefore use the entire letter; or you may feel that you only require advice on one or two points, and therefore select the appropriate paragraphs and delete everything else.

[Insert name and address of solicitors]

[Insert your own name and address]

[Date]

Dear Sirs,

The late [insert name of deceased] of [insert address]

Further to our recent meeting I have decided to instruct you on the basis of the quote given in your letter dated [insert date of letter].

I confirm that I require you to obtain a grant of [probate] [letters of administration] to the estate [and to carry out] [the conveyancing,] [your tax proposal,] [the deed of variation,] [the trust work,] [and to deal with the inheritance tax issues, including arranging payment of any inheritance tax that is due].

I also require you to:

[• look through the papers of the deceased and check them against my lists of assets and liabilities to make sure that the list is correct]

[• confirm that my list of assets correctly states whether the assets are the sole property of the deceased or jointly owned]

[• confirm that my list of beneficiaries is correct and that I have correctly stated what they should receive from the estate]

If you are planning on carrying out the third stage yourself...

[• provide written advice on whether any adverse consequences could arise from cashing in and transferring the assets and whether any action should be considered to mitigate capital gains tax before I proceed]

If you are planning on carrying out the fourth stage yourself...

[• provide written advice on whether I can safely pay all the debts from the money that I obtain from the banks etc]

[• provide written advice on whether a deed of variation or tax planning arrangement should be considered; and, if so, providing a quote for carrying out the deed of variation/tax planning]

[• provide written advice as to whether there are any issues not referred to above which could complicate administering the estate and paying the beneficiaries, such as lifetime trusts, conditional gifts or will trusts (if any) I have failed to consider (this is not intended as an exhaustive list of possible issues)]

[• provide written advice on the following: [list the issues, if any, that require explanation]]

[• advise me in writing of any enquiries I should make that I have not already made, e.g. for the purposes of completing the forms to obtain probate.]

I look forward to hearing from you in the near future.

Thank you for your assistance.

Yours faithfully,

....[signature]

Precedent letter 23 – account closure letter to bank/building society

Note

It is not intended that this entire letter should be used in all cases. You are encouraged to use only those paragraphs which apply to your circumstances. You may feel that you require advice at every stage and therefore use the entire letter; or you may feel that you only require advice on one or two points, and therefore select the appropriate paragraphs and delete everything else.

[Insert name and address of bank/building society]

[Insert your own name and address]

[Date]

Dear Sirs,

The late [insert name of deceased] of [insert address]

Account number(s): [insert account details]

Further to previous correspondence, I enclose an office copy of the grant to the estate together with your withdrawal form fully completed and signed. Please close the account and forward a cheque for the sum due to my address, made payable to me in my capacity as the personal representative of the estate.

Please include information about the interest paid on the account from the date of death until the date of account closure, including information as to the amount (if any) of tax paid at source.

I look forward to hearing from you in the near future.

Thank you for your assistance.

Yours faithfully,

....[signature]

N.B. Remember to complete and enclose the withdrawal form and to enclose the probate.

Precedent letter 24 – letter to insurance company to cash policy

[Insert name and address of insurance company]

[Insert your own name and address]

[Date]

Dear Sirs,

The late [insert name of deceased] of [insert address]

Policy number(s): [insert policy details]

Further to previous correspondence, I enclose an office copy of the grant to the estate together with your claim form fully completed and signed. Please cash the policy and forward a cheque for the sum due to my address, made payable to me in my capacity as the personal representative of the estate.

Please include information about the interest paid on the policy from the date of death until the date of encashment, including information as to the amount (if any) of tax paid at source.

I look forward to hearing from you in the near future.

Thank you for your assistance.

Yours faithfully,

....[signature]

N.B. Remember to complete and enclose the claim form and to enclose the probate.

Precedent letter 25 – letter to stockbrokers to sell shares

[Insert name and address of stockbrokers]

[Insert your own name and address]

[Date]

Dear Sirs,

The late [insert name of deceased] of [insert address]

Shares in [insert name(s) of company or companies] plc

Further to previous correspondence, I enclose an office copy of the grant to the estate together with the share certificate(s).

Please arrange to sell the shares as soon as possible.

Please forward a cheque for the sum due to my address, made payable to me in my capacity as the personal representative of the estate.

I look forward to hearing from you in the near future.

Thank you for your assistance.

Yours faithfully,

....[signature]

N.B. Remember to enclose the share certificates and the probate; the stockbrokers will reply to your letter by sending you a document for signature and return, before carrying out the sale of the shares.

Precedent letter 26 – letter to stockbrokers to transfer shares

[Insert name and address of stockbrokers]

[Insert your own name and address]

[Date]

Dear Sirs,

The late [insert name of deceased] of [insert address]

Shares in [insert name(s) of company or companies] plc

Further to previous correspondence, I enclose an office copy of the grant to the estate together with the share certificate(s). Please arrange to transfer the shares to [insert name of beneficiary] as soon as possible.

I look forward to hearing from you in the near future.

Thank you for your assistance.

Yours faithfully,

....[signature]

N.B. Remember to enclose the share certificates and the probate; the stockbrokers will reply to your letter by sending you a document for signature and return, before carrying out the transfer of the shares.

Precedent letter 27 – letter to insurance company to cash pension policy

[Insert name and address of insurance company]

[Insert your own name and address]

[Date]

Dear Sirs,

The late [insert name of deceased] of [insert address]

Pension plan number(s): [insert pension plan details]

Further to previous correspondence, I enclose an office copy of the grant to the estate together with your claim form fully completed and signed.

Please cash the plan and forward a cheque for the sum due to my address, made payable to me in my capacity as the personal representative of the estate.

Please include information about the interest paid on the plan from the date of death until the date of encashment, including information as to the amount (if any) of tax paid at source.

I look forward to hearing from you in the near future.

Thank you for your assistance.

Yours faithfully,

....[signature]

N.B. Remember to complete and enclose the claim form and the probate.

Precedent letter 28 – letter to employer claiming arrears of wages/salary

[Insert name and address of employer company]

[Insert your own name and address]

[Date]

Dear Sirs,

The late [insert name of deceased] of [insert address]

National Insurance no: [insert NI number]

Payroll no: [insert payroll no]

Further to previous correspondence, I enclose an office copy of the grant to the estate.

Please forward a cheque for the sum due to the estate in respect of arrears of pay to my address, made payable to me in my capacity as the personal representative of the estate.

I look forward to hearing from you in the near future.

Thank you for your assistance.

Yours faithfully,

....[signature]

N.B. Remember to enclose the probate.

Precedent letter 29 – letter to pay creditor

[Insert name and address of creditor/company]

[Insert your own name and address]

[Date]

Dear Sirs,

The late [insert name of deceased] of [insert address]

[Customer reference no: / Invoice no:] [insert ref or invoice no]

Further to previous correspondence, I enclose a cheque in the sum of £[insert amount] made payable to [insert payee]. Please acknowledge receipt and confirm that this settles the liability in full and there are no further debts owed by the estate to [you / your company].

I look forward to hearing from you in the near future.

Thank you for your assistance.

Yours faithfully,

....[signature]

N.B. Remember to enclose the cheque.

Precedent letter 30 – letter to beneficiary advising of six-month delay

[Insert name and address of beneficiary]

[Insert your own name and address]

[Date]

Dear [insert name of beneficiary]

The late [insert name of deceased] of [insert address]

Further to previous correspondence, I am writing to inform you that it will still be at least another six months before I can distribute to you the [item / money] that you are due from the estate.

This is because the law states that a personal representative can only distribute an estate with the confidence that he will be safe from all personal liability if he waits for a period of six months from the issue of probate to the estate.

I do not want to delay matters, but under the circumstances I feel that I have no option.

I will contact you again as soon as the six-month time limit has expired.

Thank you for your patience.

Yours sincerely,

....[signature]

Precedent letter 31 – letter to beneficiary to pay a specific sum of money from a will

[Insert name and address of beneficiary]

[Insert your own name and address]

[Date]

Dear [insert name of beneficiary]

The late [insert name of deceased] of [insert address] – legacy

Further to previous correspondence, I enclose a cheque in the sum of £[insert amount] together with a copy of this letter which is an exact duplicate. Please sign and date the duplicate letter where indicated, then return it for my records.

Thank you for your assistance.

Yours sincerely,

....[signature]

I [insert name of beneficiary] acknowledge receipt of the above sum representing payment in full of the legacy I am due from the estate.

....[signature]

Date...............................

N.B. Remember to enclose the cheque and a duplicate copy of the letter.

Precedent letter 32 – letter circulating estate accounts to a residuary beneficiary

[Insert name and address of beneficiary]

[Insert your own name and address]

[Date]

Dear [insert name of beneficiary]

The late [insert name of deceased] of [insert address] – legacy

Further to previous correspondence, I am writing to inform you that it should now be possible to pay the beneficiaries and wind up the estate.

I enclose two copies of estate accounts for your reference, providing information about the sums of money that have been handled on behalf of the estate. Please sign one copy of the accounts and return it to me, and retain the other for your own records. I will then pay you the sum due to you as shown in the estate accounts, together with any interest that may have accrued in the meantime.

I look forward to hearing from you.

Thank you for your assistance.

Yours sincerely,

....[signature]

N.B. Remember to enclose the estate accounts.

Precedent letter 33 – letter to beneficiary to pay a share of residue

[Insert name and address of beneficiary]

[Insert your own name and address]

[Date]

Dear [insert name of beneficiary]

The late [insert name of deceased] of [insert address] – legacy

Further to previous correspondence, I enclose a cheque in the sum of £[insert amount] together with a copy of this letter which is an exact duplicate. Please sign and date the duplicate letter where indicated, then return it for my records.

I also enclose a form R185 to assist you with your personal tax affairs.

Thank you for your assistance.

Yours sincerely,

....[signature]

I [insert name of beneficiary] acknowledge receipt of the above sum representing payment in full of the residue that I am due from the estate.

....[signature]

Date.................................

N.B. Remember to enclose the cheque and a duplicate copy of the letter.

Appendix 3

Specimen of Estate Accounts

The Estate of the Late Mrs Example

Assets

Capital Account*	£
House	220,000.00
Bank	12,500.00
Life Policy	7,500.00
Shares ISA	10,500.00
Cash	150.00
Car	4,000.00
Total:	254,650.00

Less:

Liabilities	£
Funeral bill	3,200.00
HMCS Probate fees	95.00
Conveyancing fees (as per attached statement)	528.75
House Insurance	250.00
Utility bills	127.00
Total:	4,200.75 (4,200.75)

Balance transferred to distribution account: £250,449.25

---

* The value of the assets at the date of death.

Income account**	Tax £	Net £
Bank	16.00	64.00
Executorship account	12.50	50.00

Balance transferred to distribution account: £114.00

Distribution account

	£
Balance from capital account:	250,449.25
Balance from income account:	114.00
Total available for distribution:	250,563.25

Legacies

Anne-Marie	£100.00
Jacob	£100.00

Residue

Peter 1/2	£125,181.62
Joanne 1/2	£125,181.62

Total distributed: £250,563.25

(Note: if you make a mistake in the accounts and then rely on them for the distribution you could cause loss to someone).

** The income received since the date of death.

Index

A

accounts 125-6

agricultural interests 40
    precedent letter 86-7

annuity
    precedent letter 96

assets 34-43, 53-4

Association of Contentious Trust and Probate Specialists (ACTAPS) 14

B

bank account(s) 34-5, 53
    precedent letter(s) 88, 114-5

beneficiaries 45, 58-9
    precedent letter(s) 101-7, 121-4

business interests 40
    precedent letter 86-7

C

capital gains tax (CGT) 43-4

conveyancing 6

credit card companies
    precedent letter 99

creditors (see: debts)

D

death certificate 19, 31-2

debts 5, 44, 55-7
    precedent letter(s) 100, 120

deeds of variation 16-7

distribution of estate 5, 58, 60-1 (see also: beneficiaries)
    interim distribution 62

documents 29

E

executor 25
expenses 5

F

fees 14-16, 46-52
financial advisor(s) 35
    precedent letter 86-7
flats (see: house)
funeral 30, 32
    precedent letter 84

G

gifts 19, 41-2
Grant of Letters of Administration 3

H

house
    contents 39
    insurance 28-9
    property (see: property)
    rental 29-30
    secure 28

I

income tax 42-4
inheritance tax 6, 41-2
insurance 28-9, 36
    precedent letter(s) 89, 115

J

jargon 1-2

L

N

P

S